SURVIVING GRADUATE SCHOOL PART TIME

Graduate Survival Skills

Series Editor
Bruce A. Thyer, Ph.D.
Research Professor of Social Work
University of Georgia

The volumes in this series attempt to demystify the process of earning a graduate degree. They seek to meet the need among young scholars for insights into the workings of graduate schools, from the application and admissions process through finding an academic job.

This series is targeted at readers interested in strategies for improving their experience in and with graduate school. The authors of the books come from a variety of academic disciplines, and a variety of career stages.

We invite ideas for future books in this series. Possible topics include:

> *Getting into Graduate School, Financing Your Graduate Education, Completing Your Dissertation or Thesis, Working with Your Major Professor or Advisory Committee, Maintaining a Rewarding Personal Life as a Graduate Student,* and *Handling Difficult or Sensitive Situations While in Graduate School.*

We encourage authors from all academic disciplines, and at any career stage. Potential authors can submit formal proposals (along with a current c.v.) for individual titles to the Series Editor.

SURVIVING GRADUATE SCHOOL PART TIME

Von Pittman

GRADUATE SURVIVAL SKILLS

SAGE Publications
International Educational and Professional Publisher
Thousand Oaks   London   New Delhi

For information:

SAGE Publications, Inc.
2455 Teller Road
Thousand Oaks, California 91320
E-mail: order@sagepub.com

SAGE Publications Ltd.
6 Bonhill Street
London EC2A 4PU
United Kingdom

SAGE Publications India Pvt. Ltd.
M-32 Market
Greater Kailash I
New Delhi 110 048 India

Printed in the United States of America

Library of Congress Cataloging-in-Publication Data

Pittman, Von V. (Von Vernon), 1945-
 Surviving graduate school part time / author, Von Pittman.
  p. cm. — (Surviving graduate school ; v. 1)
 Includes bibliographical references and index.
 ISBN 0-7619-0439-5 (cloth : acid free paper). — ISBN
0-7619-0440-9 (pbk. : acid free paper)
  1. Universities and colleges—United States—Graduate work—
Handbooks, manuals, etc. 2. Students, Part-time—United States—
Handbooks, manuals, etc. I. Title. II. Series.
LB2371.4.P58 1997
378.1'55—dc21   97-4584

This book is printed on acid-free paper.

97 98 99 00 01 02 03 10 9 8 7 6 5 4 3 2 1

Acquiring Editor: Jim Nageotte
Editorial Assistant: Kathleen Derby
Production Editor: Sherrise M. Purdum
Production Assistant: Denise Santoyo
Typesetter/Designer: Danielle Dillahunt
Print Buyer: Anna Chin

CONTENTS

SERIES EDITOR'S INTRODUCTION

Thy school-days frightful, desperate, wild and furious
—Shakespeare, *Richard III*

Preparing the preface for a book (or a series of books) is an enjoyable experience for an editor since it signifies that the project is virtually completed. This particular preface has a practical significance as well, in that we hope that the volumes comprising **Graduate Survival Skills** will help smooth the path of graduate education for those contemplating such a move. Entry into, and successfully completing, graduate school can be an intimidating undertaking. Many, too many, talented individuals do not even begin the journey, and the attrition rate amongst those enrolled is quite high. This represents an enormous waste of one of the world's most precious resources, human intellect.

Using a variety of disciplinary websites, word-of-mouth, and personal solicitation, a number of talented authors were recruited to prepare the initial titles in the series. After discussion with these various authors and a thorough review of their proposals, a total of six titles have been recruited for the series. In no order of precedence, these are *An African American Student's Guide to Graduate School*, *The Women's Guide to Graduate School*, *Completing Graduate School Long Distance*, *Surviving Graduate School Part-time*, and *Finding Your First Academic Job After Graduate School*. In development is *The International Student's Guide to Graduate School*.

Obviously, several titles are focused on particular student groups, while others on specialized aspects of the graduate school experience. About half of all graduate students in the United States now attend on a part-time basis. Many commute long distances or attend "class" utilizing various technological aids, such as interactive television, videotaped lectures, or electronic mail. Such pedagogical approaches pose their own strengths and limitations, and it is worthwhile to examine these in some detail. The volume on finding your first academic job is focused on those graduate students seeking careers in the college and university environment, a sizable proportion. There is no course titled "Finding a Job" in most graduate departments and professional schools, and we aim to meet the need for such a resource.

It has been two decades since I began my own graduate studies here at the University of Georgia, with five intervening years at the University of Michigan (PhD student and then an instructor), three at Florida State University (Assistant then Associate Professor), and ten here back at Georgia, eventually being promoted to Professor. The whole time I have remained in intimate contact with the graduate school experience and now regularly produce my "own" PhDs. These experiences, not unlike those of thousands of my contemporary faculty colleagues, have made me increasingly sensitive to the needs of graduate students, their personal, financial, and academic trials and tribulations. My hope, shared with those of the volume's authors, is to diminish the uncertainty of graduate school a little, to encourage qualified undergraduates and nontraditional students to seriously consider entry into graduate or professional school, and to do well once admitted.

Depending upon readers' responses to these initial volumes, additional titles may be added to the series. Suggestions of topics and potential authors are welcome and may be addressed to me.

BRUCE A. THYER
THE UNIVERSITY OF GEORGIA
ATHENS, GEORGIA

INTRODUCTION

If you are a working adult considering attending graduate school on a part-time basis, you probably want or need an advanced degree as a professional credential. It is far less likely that you want to become a professional academic or researcher. You may need a master's degree in education to maintain your teaching license, pass a salary barrier, or qualify for an administrative position. Perhaps you work for an industrial or commercial firm and have noticed that those of your colleagues who are advancing are the ones who have earned a master's in business administration (MBA) or perhaps a master's degree in engineering, agriculture, or computer science.

If you are a nurse, social worker, management-level municipal worker, or career military officer, you may have either decided, or been informed, that an advanced degree is a necessity—or at least a highly desirable asset—for advancement to the next career level. Your employer may encourage you to seek an advanced degree or perhaps may require you to do so—at least if you want a promotion.

If you are like most working adults, it probably seems as if the topic of graduate school could not have come at a worse time. You are probably already working long hours to establish your career. It is likely that you have a young family. You have almost certainly made major financial commitments, such as a home and automobile. And you may still be paying off your undergraduate student loan. In the face of such obstacles, undertaking a long-term commitment that will inevitably require the expenditure of great amounts of time, energy, emotion, and usually money can seem daunting at best, forbidding at worst.

Whether you are on the cusp of a decision about whether to enter a graduate program or have already decided to do so, this book is intended to provide you with some useful information, some advice, and a few shortcuts. At the very least, you should learn that you are not alone.

In nearly 20 years of service in the divisions of continuing education of three major state universities, I have enjoyed working with a variety of academic departments, professional schools, and colleges to develop accessible graduate programs for part-time students, mainly working adults. Whether in engineering or education, social work or nursing, I have encountered deans, department chairs, and professors who feel an obligation to advance their disciplines by providing advanced training to working professionals. And virtually all of these faculty members have come to appreciate and enjoy the contact with their "real world" counterparts.

The adult students I have encountered have also been impressive. Most of them bring not only commitment and a seriousness of purpose to the classroom but expertise and savvy as well. They teach each other and the faculty. Although it is obvious that they have altered the demographics of graduate study, in the areas in which they have entered in great numbers, they have also changed its essential nature— for the better.

I have tried to write in an informal, conversational style. In addition, I have written frankly and sometimes irreverently about how universities and their graduate programs work. I hope that neither of these choices will offend. Like all institutions devised and run by humans, universities have their share of failings and foibles. And they have resisted change more successfully than most. Overall, however, most do their jobs very well. Actually, I have always enjoyed working for universities and still consider it a privilege.

This book will begin with some background on the development of graduate school as a part-time phenomenon and the changing nature of graduate degrees, especially at the master's level. It will offer some thoughts on such practical matters as examining your choice of schools and programs, coping with the bureaucracy of universities, and financing your studies. It will also examine the possibilities of extending your access to graduate study through programs offered via several nontraditional formats, generically known as "distance education."

Last, this book will offer some highly subjective thoughts on being a working professional and a grad student simultaneously. Remember as you consider a graduate degree, lesser people than you have earned them while working at full-time jobs and—believe it or not—so have busier people. And most of them have survived as reasonable human beings. Advanced study taken while working and maintaining other commitments is never easy, but it is almost always worthwhile.

Many faculty, administrators, and student colleagues at The University of Iowa and around the country have provided information, perspective, and advice. I sincerely appreciate their help. In particular, Rachel Imes, a graduate assistant from Iowa's College of Education, did outstanding work in improving this manuscript.

I would like to dedicate this book to my wife, Joyce Zeller Pittman. Her support and interest over the course of this project have made all the difference.

1

THE ALTERNATE PATH

The ultimate goal of the educational system is to shift to the individual the burden of pursuing his education.

—John W. Gardner

Earning a graduate degree while working full time and satisfying other commitments is a demanding challenge but one that is both possible and feasible. If you make this commitment, you will not be alone. According to the Council of Graduate Schools (CGS; 1995), nearly half of all graduate students are enrolled on a part-time basis. At the master's degree level, they account for nearly 70% of all enrollments. Thus, part-time graduate students represent the norm, not the exception. Every year, approximately 150,000 part-time students earn graduate degrees.

The majority of these women and men are not preparing for a life of research and teaching within the academy. Nor are many seeking such abstract—if worthy—goals as "fulfillment" or "self-actualization." By definition, none of them are making a single-minded commitment to their studies. Instead, they decided to fit graduate study into already busy lives, along with holding jobs, managing families, and participating

1

in the lives of their communities. For them, graduate study is only one of several roles they balance. Colin Powell, who earned an MBA from George Washington University while on active duty, put his graduate experience in perspective when he said, "I was a good student, but no scholar, and a soldier before a student" (Powell, 1995, p. 149). Balancing serious commitments is not easy. The fact that others are doing it does not necessarily mean that you should. However, if you want or need an advanced degree, if you are capable of, or amenable to, making short-term sacrifices in the interest of long-term rewards—and if you can fit another major commitment of time and energy into your life and that of your family, graduate study can be feasible and rewarding. A variety of institutions, programs, and support services exist to help make such a goal a definite possibility.

GRADUATE SCHOOL: THE ELITIST IDEAL AND THE SERVICE MISSION

U.S. universities began to come into prominence in the late 19th century. For the most part, they followed the British example for undergraduate students but based their graduate programs on the research-oriented German university. Professors and intellectuals declared that universities should be centered on the liberal arts, placing the highest value on research and graduate-level teaching. The research, moreover, should be aimed not at problem solving or practical application but rather on the generation of new knowledge. Cardinal Newman (1927), in his influential *The Idea of a University*, declared "the business of a University" was the cultivation of the intellect, rather than specialized training for a trade or profession (p. 174).

The economist Thorstein Veblen (1918) declared graduate teaching and research the only real business of a university. He scorned both professional training and efforts to make higher education accessible to anyone other than fully committed students. Abraham Flexner (1930), perhaps the most influential critic of American universities in their formative years, called graduate study "by far the most meritorious part of the American university" (p. 73). His vision of graduate study was narrow. Of the professional schools, he said, only two—law and medicine—properly belonged in universities; colleges for such subjects as business and education definitely did not. Any efforts to broaden access beyond full-time students—such as providing extension or correspondence courses—would automatically lower the quality, standards, and prestige of American universities.

By the time elitist critics such as Veblen and Flexner made their observations, the reality of American universities had already passed them by. Professional schools had become prominent fixtures in even the best universities. Furthermore, due to the politics of the Progressive Era and the inception of federal funding to universities under the land grant acts, many prominent universities had developed extensive programs to serve working professionals, particularly teachers and other educators. Nonetheless, the elitist critique of American universities has had a profound and lasting influence on graduate education.

From their formative periods, the graduate colleges of U.S. universities have served as a focal point for the tension between the pragmatic and democratic service missions and the prevailing elitist ideal of the scholarly vocation. The earliest notable example of this tension came in the area of advanced training for teachers and administrators within education. In 1891, the University of California began to offer extension courses to accommodate working teachers and administrators (Rockhill, 1983). By the turn of the century, many universities had expanded accommodations to serve part-time students. This sparked an elitist backlash among the traditionalists, who considered such accommodations a corruption of what graduate study should be. As early as 1910, the Association of American Universities (AAU) began to issue reports highly critical of delivery formats designed to facilitate part-time graduate study, such as extension courses and correspondence study. A 1927 AAU report went much further, adding summer courses for teachers to its list of suspect teaching formats (Glazer, 1986, p. 9).

None of these pronouncements put an end to part-time graduate study. The need and the demand were simply too strong. But as demand grew, so did opposition. Graduate colleges imposed severe limits on the number of extension courses a student could apply to a master's degree. Most refused to accept any credits earned through correspondence study.

In an influential book on teacher education, James Conant (1963) deplored part-time graduate study. He did, however, see the value in encouraging teachers to earn master's degrees but not on a part-time basis. Teachers working full time, he said, could not do justice to a graduate program by taking classes at night, on weekends, or at off-campus sites. If school districts wanted their teachers to earn master's degrees, they should provide them with paid leaves of absence so they could do so properly, on campus, in full-time residence. Arguments like Conant's and the earlier condemnations of the AAU have not reduced the number of programs available for part-time, working adult students. Indeed, such opportunities have proliferated. But the consequences of these views endure on many campuses, making part-time study more difficult than it need be. The traditional graduate education model has resulted in restrictive policies and regulations, such as strict residency requirements, severely limited use of transfer and extension course credits, and the disallowing of some instructional formats (correspondence or other forms of distance education, for example). Many university administrators, graduate deans, and faculty councils tend to view such restrictions as "standards" that ensure quality. They rarely consider that they might be no more than practices, based mainly on nostalgia, that function as barriers—or at least annoyances—to working adults pursuing degrees on a part-time basis. Although the reality of graduate study has changed about everywhere, the mythology often remains.

THE GRADUATE CREDENTIAL

You may be a teacher who wants to become a principal, or a nurse, social worker, or librarian intent on moving up. You might be an assistant city manager determined to drop the adjective. Perhaps you are a professional engineer considering earning an MBA to move into management or a junior officer who must earn a master's degree to make the Air Force a career. Maybe you have noticed that in your company, promotions come faster for the managers with MBAs or master's degrees in agriculture. Possibly by happenstance, you find yourself working in some sort of support office on a college campus. Although you have a bachelor's degree, it has become apparent that only a graduate degree will ever enable you to move from clerical to professional status.

If you fit into any of these categories or a number of others, you are considering a graduate degree as a means of acquiring the skills and status that will open, enhance, or prolong a career. You are not interested in an apprenticeship for a career as a scholar. Instead, you want or need a professional credential. And this should not relegate you to a second-class status. Developing and providing professional credentials has become one of the chief functions of graduate colleges. Well before the beginning of this century, the U.S. public, along with many employers, had accepted the idea that diplomas represented legitimate qualifications for many occupations and professions (Brown, 1995). According to some sociologists and historians, it is this de facto certification by educational degrees that accounts for the explosive expansion of U.S. higher education in the 20th century (Labaree, 1995).

As technology and specialization have led to increasing sophistication in the professions, the demand for degrees has ratcheted up accordingly. In fields in which baccalaureate degrees once sufficed, graduate degrees now define the professional standard. Scholars have frequently debated the effects of this certification by advanced degree. One sociologist, taking a dim view of this phenomenon, which he called *credentialism,* argues that "higher education exists largely as a mechanism for providing individuals with a cultural commodity that will give them a substantial competitive edge in the pursuit of social position" (Labaree, 1995, p. xiv). Thus, education becomes little but a public subsidy for private ambition.

Other scholars, however, see the credentialing process as a sophisticated relationship between academics and the professions that benefits the larger society. Charles Anderson (1993) noted, "the stipulation of best practice, the definition of the normative culture of the profession, the certification of practitioners, are functions performed through close, deliberative collaboration between academics and professionals" (p. 155).

Whether the tacit agreement between employers and graduate and professional schools on the value of advanced degrees as a negative or positive development for the larger society is, for you, beside the point. It is not your problem. Whether or not you should undertake a graduate degree program, making the necessary accommodations to add it to your other activities, commitments, and relationships, depends entirely on your individual needs and circumstances. If you are considering the idea, I'm sure you have already begun to weigh short-term costs against long-term benefits.

THE LONG WAY:
PART-TIME STUDY

If you are contemplating earning a graduate degree as a part-time student, it will almost certainly be a master's of some sort. With the exception of the field of education, doctoral study is exceedingly rare among part-time students. At the master's level, however, the part-time student is the norm. In its most recent profile of member institutions, the CGS (1995) reported that 74% of master's students were enrolled on a part-time basis.

The master's degree, unlike a doctoral degree, is highly idiosyncratic. Due mainly to the demands for specialization in the various professions, there are hundreds of variations. For all this variety, however, the master's degree serves one of only three purposes. In the classic graduate school tradition, it can be the first formal step toward the doctorate and a life in research and teaching. In some programs, it is a classy consolation prize for those who start a PhD program but are judged by the faculty as unworthy to complete it. Most important, however, in terms of overall numbers—and for the purposes of this book—it is recognized as the most advanced academic credential available by many professions.

The nomenclature of master's degrees is ambiguous and slippery. As Judith Glazer (1986) has noted, during the 1970s, university faculties made an effort to draw a distinction between traditional research-oriented degrees, intended for career academics, and professional or "practitioner" degrees. The former have frequently been called *traditional, academic,* or *liberal arts* master's degrees, whereas the latter are usually known as *practitioners'* master's degrees. For the purposes of this book, I will use the terms *academic master's* and *professional master's* to differentiate between these two general classes of degrees.

Glazer (1986) offered a useful distinction between the two types of degrees. The professional master's, she said, is "highly differentiated, and its content and structure are based on more utilitarian and measurable objectives, directed toward more immediate outcomes" (p. 25).

Robert Peters (1992) offers another useful way of drawing a distinction between master's programs. Some require a candidate to produce a thesis at the end of his or her program, some do not. For the most part, the "thesis master's" would correspond to the academic diploma and the nonthesis version to the professional degree. But this is not always the case. For example, in some programs, notably in colleges of education, a student may choose to take a master's program on either a thesis or nonthesis basis. In some professional master's programs, in some universities, theses are still required. Most working adults enroll in professional master's programs. Most do not write theses. The Office of Education Research and Improvement (1985) categorized 84% of the total master's degrees awarded in the United States as professional, and 16% as liberal arts. This profile is consistent with the practices of part-time students. In a more recent survey of graduate education, the Illinois Board of Higher Education (IBHE; 1996) counted more than 600 master's programs offered off campus (virtually all were designed for working adults attending part time). Seventy-five percent were in three fields— business, education, and engineering. More than half of the master's degrees awarded were in two fields, business and education. The addition of health professions, public administration, and engineering raised the total to more than two thirds of master's degrees (IBHE, 1996). By any measure, the dominance of professional master's degrees is overwhelming.

The professional master's clearly has become the relevant terminal degree and premier credential in most professions outside academia. A number of factors have contributed to this development. First, many professional master's degrees do not require any specific undergraduate preparation other than a bachelor's degree. Therefore, a master's degree can be a reasonably efficient means of effecting a major career shift.

My own experience provides an example. In the 1970s, I was working toward a PhD in history. Due to the gross overproduction of doctoral degrees in most areas of the humanities and social sciences at that time, many young PhD candidates realized that they (we) were not going to become professors in our chosen academic fields. In the history program in which I was enrolled, some of us decided that we had better prepare as quickly as possible for other lines of work. Several of us did so by enrolling in professional master's programs, either just after completing the PhD or while working on our history dissertations. Either way, we were truly part-time students. A couple of friends took the master's in library science, one the master's in public administration, and two of us the master's in education (MEd).

The point is that all of us had our undergraduate and master's degrees in history; we were able to enter these programs with neither training nor formal education in the relevant fields.

The MBA is probably the premier example of a professional master's degree that is open to people from virtually all undergraduate majors (however, it may be necessary for candidates to take some business-related prerequisite courses as part of their programs of study). There are, of course, some fields in which this flexibility does not apply. In engineering and nursing, to cite two obvious examples, graduate work builds directly on undergraduate preparation.

The wide variety of master's degrees, many quite specific in content, provides another explanation for their suitability as professional credentials. *Peterson's Annual Guide to Graduate Study* (1985) lists 667 master's degree titles. Many are quite specific; some are even customized for specific corporate audiences. To a large extent, the range of professional master's options demonstrates that many institutions of higher education have accommodated the marketplace, some quite aggressively. Thus, the professional master's diploma usually represents a certification of specific skills and knowledge. It is not merely a hoop to jump through or a certificate to hang on the wall.

Its immediate utility is the premier reason for the popularity of the professional master's degree. And earning it on a part-time basis is a reasonable goal and a manageable task for many adults working full time.

THE DOCTORATE:
THE REALLY HARD WAY

None of the factors working in favor of the professional master's apply at the doctoral level. Based on theory building and sophisticated research rather than utilitarian knowledge and applied skills, the doctorate rarely has value as a professional credential outside of the academy or other research-based employment. A few exceptions to this principle do exist, of course, such as the doctor of psychology (PsyD), doctor of pharmacy (PharmD), and other so-called professional (i.e., not academic) doctoral degrees.

The typical doctoral program of study may take 3 to 5 years, or more, of full-time work. To say that doubling or tripling such a commitment presents a formidable obstacle for part-timers would be a gross understatement. Furthermore, the duration of a doctoral program is only one problem. Students who are able to take only evening classes have limited access to labs and libraries. Even in university libraries, which normally keep extended hours, such critical services as the reference desk and interlibrary loan often shut down at night. The special collections room, critical to some disciplines, is rarely open after office hours.

Last, the monetary costs of doctoral study are considerable. Except for employer support, part-time students seldom receive assistance. They cannot teach or work as research assistants. Academic departments reserve their support for full-time students. And even if they did not, few working adults could fit a teaching assistantship into their schedules. Employers rarely reimburse tuition at this level. In almost all cases, years of tuition costs would come out of the student's own bank account.

If all of this were not difficult enough, another factor makes the part-time doctoral student a rarity. Such a creature is alien to the culture of the PhD. The programs simply do not fit. Most have impossible research requirements and many mandate service as a teaching assistant. Even such elementary conveniences as courses scheduled at night are not generally available. And all of this is made worse by administrative hurdles. At many institutions, residency requirements explicitly block part-time doctoral study. For example, in most departments at The University of Iowa, a doctoral student must register for a full-time load, in residence, for at least two semesters. Such requirements represent the norm, not the exception, in conventional doctoral programs, and they clearly fit neither the needs nor the lifestyles of most full-time working professionals.

There is one important exception to these generalizations. Many working administrators, and a few teachers, in the K-12 and community college systems seek either an EdD or PhD in education. They can often fulfill their residency requirements in intensive summer sessions or through some other specially tailored solution. The extreme duration of a program, although still daunting, is feasible and socially acceptable among the students' professional colleagues and peer group.

Doctoral students in education usually have access to the facilities and research materials needed for a thesis or dissertation. Indeed, many base their research on problems and issues related to their places of work. Such topics as student retention, student or faculty satisfaction, and faculty development can be researched, in large part, on the job, often in a format or manner that can complement one's work. And education, as an academic discipline, is uniquely suited to part-time study. This is not to say that doctoral work in education is easy. Indeed, it can be quite demanding. However, in contrast to science and technology and the humanities, a part-time student can find access to doctoral programs—with night classes and the like—and survive the culture. And even then, most part-time students who pursue the doctorate are not planning a lifetime of research; they do not intend to work as professors. Like most master's students, they are seeking a professional credential.

PROS AND CONS
OF PART-TIME STUDY

The rough standard for the traditional master's degree is a year of full-time study, plus a thesis. The time frame is usually roughly the same for the nonthesis version of the professional master's, but this varies from place to place and program to program. Some programs require as little as 32 semester hours, whereas others require in excess of 60 semester hours. For the part-time student, a 1-year program generally translates to 2 or 3 years, depending on an individual's course load. Although a 3-year commitment of time and energy can seem forbidding, for most people, it usually seems within the realm of possibility.

As we have seen, the professional master's represents by far the most accessible and serviceable path toward a graduate degree for part-time students. However, it is not necessarily trouble free and user friendly.

Its practical approach to the curriculum does not mean it is academically less rigorous. Nor should it be. And for the part-time student, many of the traditional barriers and hassles remain. Graduate deans have traditionally considered themselves and their staffs as gatekeepers, defenders of the academic faith, upholders of the sacred standards. Indeed, establishing and maintaining a universitywide standard is the mission of the graduate dean. Their zeal is commendable.

However, universities change slowly, probably more slowly than any other institution. Too often, deans and other administrators, and the faculty, equate habits with standards. *Quality* frequently means "the way it was when we were graduate students." The traditional design of graduate study remains, with entrenched regulations and policies that can annoy and even hinder the working adults who make up the bulk of part-time students. Although such problems occur much less frequently in programs specifically designed for working adults, the cases in which they are totally absent are rare. I will address some of these barriers in detail in Chapter 5.

So far, I have alluded to a number of factors that can make part-time graduate study difficult. Some are structural, some are human; some are intentional, some are unwitting; some are unique to particular institutions, some are generic and omnipresent. Most are real; a few are imagined. Taken together, these factors make up a significant body of disadvantages facing adults who want to earn a degree while working full time. This is not a one-sided story, however.

Some of the apparent disadvantages of part-time study have redeeming features. Furthermore, part-time study offers some substantial advantages over the full-time version. This book's controlling cliché is the expression, "Life is an endless series of trade-offs." (Some books have controlling metaphors; this one has a controlling cliché.) Consequently, it would be a good idea to survey the comparative advantages and disadvantages, real and purported, of both modes of graduate study.

Part-time graduate students, especially those who are fully employed, will always have fewer options than full-time students. The part-time student can take only those programs that fit his or her schedule. This usually means nights or weekends, but it can also mean courses offered at off-campus sites or even distance education programs in which course work is offered asynchronously. No university could offer its full range of programs under these strictures, even if it so desired.

Within the available programs, part-time students will also have fewer options for course work. Again, colleges and universities cannot offer as many courses at night, at remote sites, or via distance education formats. Naturally, programs must provide all necessary courses to meet the total degree requirements. However, the variety of core courses available and the range of electives may be seriously limited. In many cases, the word *elective* has no real meaning. The student may be required to take every course offered, not because of curricular limitations but because nothing else will be made available. Particularly if you enter a program run on a so-called cohort basis, you may have no choices at all. You may have to take each and every course offered in the program.

In most cases, however, students who strongly wish to vary their course work have some options. Most master's programs allow in the neighborhood of 6 to 9 semester hours—or the equivalent in quarter hours—of transfer credit. It should be possible to take a course or two, either an elective or perhaps a methods course, from another university.

The University of Iowa's off-campus Master of Arts in Higher Education program, offered via interactive television, encourages students at the remote sites to take their research methods courses or electives of particular interest from other universities. Independent study courses, designed by arrangement with program faculty, provide another means of varying course work. In some programs, such individually arranged courses are used frequently on campus. If you intend to use either transfer courses or independent study courses, you will need to ask your adviser to approve them in advance. Never take a chance on a course that might not be applicable to your program. Even more than full-time students, part-timers cannot waste time or money on any course that is not applicable to their programs of study.

There is no question that limited access to the faculty represents a distinct disadvantage for part-time students. Most professors—even those who teach night courses and at off-campus sites—hold their office hours only during the workday. If any of your professors are adjunct appointees, as many are in some programs designed for evening and off-campus students, they may have no office hours at all and perhaps no office. They may have little familiarity with advising work. Thus, although such professors might have excellent command of their subject matter, they may know little about overall program rules and procedures.

To deal with the problem of access to faculty, some programs—especially those run in conjunction with continuing education offices—have begun to try to work out alternatives to traditional office hours. Specified telephone office hours are one obvious, and frequent, alternative. Some schools, such as Central Michigan University, provide special training in advising and programmatic areas for adjunct professors who work in off-campus programs.

Access to competent advising is closely related to faculty access. Unfortunately, academic advising is the primary weakness in most programs designed for part-time students. As with academic office hours, advising is pretty much a day job at most universities. Off-campus centers frequently provide little or no advising. The same can be true of distance education programs.

The administrators of many programs aimed at part-time students use the lockstep nature of the curriculum, particularly in the cohort model, as an excuse for sketchy or limited advising. Because there is so little variation in the course work, with few choices to make, the argument goes, little advising is needed. Although there is some truth to this line of reasoning, it is not sufficient. There are always questions about transfer credit, for example. And despite the rigidity of the cohort model, students occasionally must drop out for a term. Good advising services try to find alternative means of accommodating them.

In recent years, the advising situation in evening, off-campus, and distance education programs has been improving. Advisers—both professional and faculty—often travel to off-campus sites for orientation and advising sessions. More schools are making use of modern technology—such as interactive audio, video, or computer conferencing in advising. Some programs—and here again, Central Michigan is a leader—provide local professional advisers at selected off-campus sites. Often, they are the same people who teach in the programs.

One of the most difficult problems of access has to do with university offices and services not directly related to instruction: the registrar, the graduate dean's office, financial aid offices, libraries, and, worst of all, the parking office. At most universities, these offices are still run on an 8-to-5 basis. Many universities have found it far easier to provide classes and programs to part-time students than to arrange for support services on a par with those taken for granted on campus during the day. Although change is taking place, the pace is often slow. Ironically, the larger and more prestigious the university, the less accommodating to part-time graduate students it is likely to be.

▓ Access to the Campus Culture

The issue I most frequently hear university professors and administrators cite as a disadvantage of part-time study is that students have insufficient access to the collegiate culture. Many of my colleagues believe that part-time students miss an invaluable set of experiences by not immersing themselves in campus life. This argument is not without merit. Life on campus is enjoyable, it is usually stimulating, and it can sometimes be exciting. But it is not essential. I would argue that the absence of a residential experience does not diminish the value of either a graduate diploma or the education it represents. No one has ever proven—or could prove—that recipients of a given master's degree are lesser nurses, engineers, managers, or school superintendents because they missed some of the ancillary pleasures of the university culture.

It is true that by going to school part time, by making it a matter only of courses and study, you will not get to associate with your peers to the degree that you might if you were in full-time residence. Most of your day will be devoted to your job and family. However, as the following examples demonstrate, the brevity of your time in class and on campus does not necessarily mean that you cannot benefit from your contact with other students.

About 30 years ago, Iowa established a system of community colleges. Roughly a decade later, many of their administrators began doctoral programs on a part-time basis. Several earned their degrees in a program based largely on weekend classes at The University of Iowa. Now, they are senior officers—chancellors, presidents and vice presidents, and deans—in the community college system. The network that grew out of their association in graduate school proved useful immediately and has continued to benefit not only them but the community college system and the university as well.

Camaraderie within classes consisting of part-timers is not unknown. One of my colleagues earned her doctorate through the weekend program mentioned earlier. Within each class, she remembers, the students divided the readings that had been placed on reserve in the library. Each checked out his or her share, then made enough photocopies for all the other students. By the beginning of the second week of class, each student had a complete file of all the reserved readings. This teamwork saved all of them hours of photocopying (which is really the only way part-time students can use the reserve shelf) and extra trips to the library. Furthermore, my colleague tells me, cooperating on this task initiated a team spirit that survived not only individual courses but the program cohort as well.

Along with two colleagues, I recently completed teaching a course via two-way, interactive television. We had students at seven sites in Iowa, ranging from Sioux City, on the Missouri River, to the Quad Cities on the Mississippi. We had our largest group in Spencer, a small town in the lightly populated northwestern part of the state, where few graduate programs have ever been offered. The group of 10 students there became incredibly close. Through means I do not yet know, they selected a leader who called with all of their questions about such routine matters as test schedules, report deadlines, and the like. They arranged to take the GREs together. When a snowstorm hit on testing day, one of them confirmed the fact that the test was canceled and started a "phone tree" to notify all the others. To determine just how this "snowout" would affect their admissions process, they selected one person to call and find out. When they needed last-minute handouts, we had to fax only one set. The person who received it made copies and delivered them to all of her classmates. All in all, I have never seen such teamwork or camaraderie in any other graduate class.

Your contact with other students can be rich and rewarding in ways unknown to full-time students. The opportunity to meet people who are already well established in your profession, on an equal footing, serves as just one example of how student contacts can have long-term benefits.

▓ A Different Culture

Part-time students frequently find it difficult, if not impossible, to take advantage of the "extras" of academic life, events such as guest lectures, faculty receptions, departmental softball, and the like. This is especially true for programs offered off-campus. But even if you go to classes on campus, most such functions will be held during the working day. And even if they are held in the evening, you will often be in class or studying.

That lack of access to such events is a disadvantage of part-time study is undeniable. They can be intellectually stimulating, politically advantageous, or just fun. However, missing them does not constitute a tragedy. They simply are not as important to you as they are to your full-time student counterparts.

As a working adult, you will not face the same pressures as full-time students. Although you probably intend to enhance your position or status within your current profession or perhaps to break through into another area, your professional problems are not of the same magnitude as those of full-time students nearing the end of their programs. You are employed; they are not. These folks need to find the "right" job before graduation or shortly thereafter. Or if not, they are probably applying for acceptance into a PhD program. In either case, academic politics apply. Thus, being seen at seminars, receptions, and the like and making a good impression is critical to their future. In fact, they may be survival tactics.

Most of the guidebooks on succeeding in grad school stress the importance of academic politics. And, for the full-time student, the books are right. Things such as the dynamics between students and their advisers and between any student's adviser and the rest of the faculty can have a considerable impact. It is a cliché that academic politics are so nasty because the stakes are so low. But for full-time graduate students, the stakes are not low; they can determine one's entire future. This kind of game playing and general mean-spiritedness explains why Peters (1992) calls grad school "a ritual humiliation in which novice academics are initiated into their respective disciplines" (p. 6). Here, part-time graduate students in professional master's programs enjoy a definite advantage. For them, academic politics is rarely a concern.

The part-time student is seldom under pressure to publish, again giving him or her an edge over full-time students. For the latter group, competition for appointments to prestigious PhD programs and for academic jobs is fierce—as it has been for many years. How-to books on graduate school generally advise students to begin thinking about scholarly publication from day one. Throughout one's program, they say, every project should be aimed toward a research program that will produce a book or an article in a refereed journal before graduation.

As a part-time student, most likely in a professional master's program, you may not have to face such pressures. This is not to say that you should not do research and write for publication. In fact, I believe that most professional fields could benefit from more writing and publication from practitioners. The point, however, is that you will not likely be forced to do this while taking classes. Although you will have to divide your time between your job, family, and studies, you will not have to enter this highly competitive area until and unless you have the time and inclination to do so.

Graduate school is expensive. Neither part-time nor full-time students can escape this reality. But in this area also, the part-timer usually has the advantage. Most graduate without incurring major debts or forgoing their incomes. This topic is further explored in Chapter 6.

Graduate school is demanding, stimulating, challenging, and expensive. These adjectives apply for all students. Whether a student attends full or part time does not determine the worth of a graduate degree. Full-time study is not inherently superior nor part-time by definition inferior. This is particularly true when considering the type of degree now commonly known as the professional master's. Although full-time study has its advantages, so does earning a degree while working in a career. In particular, where academic politics and paying the bills are concerned, part-time study has a definite edge.

REFERENCES

Anderson, C. (1993). *Prescribing the life of the mind: An essay on the purpose of the university, the aims of liberal education, the competence of citizens, and the cultivation of practical reason.* Madison, WI: University of Wisconsin Press.

Brown, D. K. (1995). *Degrees of control: A sociology of educational expansion and occupational credentialism.* New York: Teachers College Press.

Conant, J. B. (1963). *The education of American teachers.* New York: McGraw-Hill.

Council of Graduate Schools, Office of Information Services. (1995). *A profile of CGS institutions, 1993: A comparative listing of CGS members by graduate enrollment and degrees conferred.* Washington, DC: Author.

Flexner, A. (1930). *Universities: American, English, German.* London: Oxford University Press.

Glazer, J. (1986). *The master's degree: Tradition, diversity, innovation.* Washington, DC: Association for the Study of Higher Education.

Illinois Board of Higher Education. (1996). *Graduate education in Illinois higher education: A reexamination of practice and policy.* Unpublished report.

Labaree, D. F. (1995). Forward. In D. K. Brown, *Degrees of control: A sociology of educational expansion and occupational credentialism* (ix-xiv). New York: Teachers College Press.

Newman, Cardinal J. H. (1927). *The idea of a university: Defined and illustrated* (D. M. O'Connell, Ed.). Chicago, IL: Loyola University Press.

Office of Education Research and Improvement. (1985). *Bachelor's, master's, and doctorates conferred, by field, 1982-83.* Unpublished data. Washington, DC: Office of Education Research and Improvement.

Peters, R. L. (1992). *Getting what you came for: The smart student's guide to earning a master's or a PhD.* New York: Noonday.

Peterson's Annual Guide to Graduate Study. (1985). Princeton, NJ: Peterson's Guides.

Powell, C. (with Persico, J.). (1995). *My American journey.* New York: Ballantine.

Rockhill, K. (1983). *Academic excellence and public service: A history of university extension in California.* New Brunswick, NJ: Transaction Books.

Veblen, T. (1918). *The theory of the leisure class: An economic study of institutions.* New York: B. W. Huebsch.

2

SELECTING A PROGRAM

When you come to a fork in the road, take it.
—Yogi Berra

The economy, stupid.
—James Carville

Remember the controlling cliché of this book: Life is an endless series of trade-offs. But like many bromides, this one is not only true, it is useful. Selecting a graduate program usually involves major trade-offs involving program quality, costs, reputation, format, accessibility, and other factors. As you consider these tradeoffs, remember James Carville's famous admonition to candidate Bill Clinton's campaign staff in 1992. When Carville posted the sign that said, "The economy, stupid," he wanted to emphasize the primacy of economic issues and to warn against being distracted by lesser matters. In selecting a graduate program, the institution is the primary factor. Nothing else is as important. Are you confident that the school you are considering offers the skills and knowledge you need? Will you be proud to be an alumnus? Will you consider the time, effort, and money expended on a degree from this institution well spent?

As you begin to think about these questions, you may gradually become aware of one of the sorry probabilities that needs to be factored into your decision. Generally, the greater the reputation of the university, the less responsive it is likely to be to the needs of adult part-time graduate students. In most of the premier state and private universities, the classic research-oriented doctoral model of graduate school still prevails. There are some exceptions to this generalization, however. For example, in many major universities, the colleges of business have withdrawn their MBA programs from the graduate college and have tailored them to their specific audiences. You need to determine how student-friendly a program is, then decide just how important that factor is to you.

In the discussion to follow, I am assuming regional accreditation as an absolute minimum standard. Furthermore, in most curricular areas, you may also want to check into specialized accreditation. For example, in the case of the MBA, schools accredited by the American Assembly of Collegiate Schools of Business (AACSB) are generally considered the most prestigious. It is possible, however, that MBA programs not accredited by the AACSB might offer advantages—such as location and length of program—that would justify a trade-off.

Whereas specialized accreditation is a trade-off issue, regional accreditation is not. If you are considering enrolling in a program from an institution that is not accredited by one of the six regional agencies or is not a candidate for accreditation, I advise you to put this book down now. It will be of no further use to you. A listing of regional and specialized accrediting agencies is given in Appendix A.

MAJOR FACTORS IN
PROGRAM SELECTION

In determining which institution is best for you, several factors come into play. First, what schools provide what you want and need, both in terms of academic quality and an acceptable credential? What is the reputation of each program and school? How important is that to you? Is the program you want accessible? Actually, accessibility will usually be the major determining factor, or at least the largest single factor, in making your choice. Accessibility involves not only geography, but scheduling, costs, and your admissibility. As you consider accessibility, the compromises—or trade-offs—will begin.

▓ Accessibility

Location is undoubtedly the most important factor when working adults choose professional master's degree programs. A study by the American Library Association, which accredits library and information science graduate programs, examined the issue of program selection among master's students. Both full-time and part-time students listed "location" as the most important factor in making their choice. However, whereas 59% of full-time students gave this reason, 77% of part-time students chose it. It is interesting that for their second choice, full-time students selected "availability of financial assistance," whereas part-timers chose "openness to working adults" (McCook & Moen, 1992). For them, openness to adults, like location, was an issue of access.

If you live in a large population area and if the degree you want is a fairly common one, such as the MBA or MEd, you should have a number of choices. Graduate programs in such areas as library science are considerably harder to find. If you live in a lightly populated or remote area, you may have to settle for a program that either is more generic than you would prefer or doesn't quite match your interests.

The department I teach in offers a master's program in higher education, via interactive television, at seven sites throughout Iowa. Most of the students are employees of community colleges or small private colleges who need a master's degree for any further promotion. For the most part, the towns in which our College of Education is offering this program are not Iowa's major population centers. Our largest enrollment, in fact, is in a very lightly populated area where the only postsecondary institutions are two small community colleges.

The area of concentration in this program is continuing education. Many of our remote students would have preferred another concentration, such as administrative practices or policy studies. Some might have preferred another institution, in fact. But because this is the first graduate program in education to have been offered in their areas, a large number of employees at the community colleges have chosen to take it. They need the master's degree as a credential, and they cannot leave homes and jobs to pursue it. In cases like this, accessibility of the program compensates for the lack of curricular preferences. This phenomenon also occurs frequently in social work and nursing, in which several "tracks" may be available on campus, but only one is offered off campus.

Some states limit access to graduate programs as a matter of economic and political policy. Normally, such policies are designed to prevent public universities from opening off-campus programs in areas of high population or significant demand (or both). There are a number of variations on this theme of "turf wars." For example, a regulatory bureaucracy might prevent two public universities from competing for the same audience. Just as often, however, the regulatory agencies forbid public universities from opening programs in areas served by private institutions. The purported reason for such policies is to save the taxpayers' money by preventing so-called unnecessary duplication. Often, this is a specious argument, however, because many public institutions run their off-campus operations on a self-sustaining funding model. In other words, student tuition covers all costs.

The primary effect—and often the overt intent—of such policies is to protect universities located in a given geographic area from competition with programs originating from more distant institutions. Thus, one institution can be given a monopoly on certain programs within a fixed population area. People who need those programs thus have fewer, if any, choices in terms of faculty quality, accessibility of offerings, curriculum, and above all, tuition cost. In effect, such policies allow citizens in some parts of a state to benefit from public education while blocking it for residents of other areas. Such policies are a form of protectionism. Most often, they protect private colleges from lower-cost programs offered by public institutions. This, of course, is what they are intended to do. Because off-campus programs are normally intended for part-time students, this group pays the price.

The days of such regulatory policies are probably numbered, however. New distance education formats are rendering them unenforceable. States can prevent their citizens from attending their own public institutions, but they cannot forbid them to enroll in programs offered via the Internet or other distance education formats.

Potential students who have genuine access problems may wish to consider programs offered via distance education. More and more people are doing so. New programs from good universities are developing rapidly. Locating and evaluating reputable and effective programs offered through distance education will be dealt with at length in Chapter 3.

▓ Admissibility

No program has any worth if you are not admissible. Geographic accessibility and cost no longer have meaning. Therefore, your evaluation of universities and programs should include serious consideration of this factor. First, do you have an undergraduate degree from a regionally accredited college or university? This question sounds so obvious as to be silly. However, I've been involved in establishing and administering graduate programs of all types at two major state universities, and the question comes up fairly often. If you don't have a bachelor's degree, getting one must be your first order of business.

If you have a bachelor's degree, is it in an appropriate discipline, or does it matter? For some graduate degrees, including most in education, library science, public administration, the Master of Social Work degree, and most MBAs, there is no specific undergraduate degree requirement. Applications from people with all sorts of bachelor's degrees are welcome. For other graduate programs, such as nursing or electrical engineering, a specific undergraduate degree is required.

In reviewing the requirements of various graduate colleges and departments, carefully check for indications that you might be required to take additional courses as prerequisites to the degree program. Also, try to determine the possible value of graduate credits, in any field, that you might have previously earned.

If your undergraduate degree was in history but you now want an MBA, some programs might require you to take additional prerequisite business courses, after admission, as part of your program of study. This could expand the length of your studies considerably. Think about this as you ponder trade-offs. If you are looking at two similar programs—but one requiring you to take six or nine additional semester hours to meet the prerequisites, the other not—the difference in time and costs could be a decisive factor.

Have you ever earned any graduate credits? If so, how long ago did you do so? Perhaps you made a false start in another field a few years ago. Or, if you are a teacher, you might have taken a workshop or summer course that offered graduate credit. Even if these courses are from an area other than the one you are now going into, you might be able to use them. For example, one of my advisees in the higher education program had previously taken some courses in social work. Our department allowed her to use six of those hours as electives in her program of study. Occasionally, to encourage interdisciplinary study, advisers and departments will allow courses from other areas to be used as part of the concentration requirement.

Although you should be prepared to make an argument for the curricular relevance of using credits earned before admission, their value extends further. Each hour of previously earned credit will shorten the duration of your program of study, at a considerable financial savings. A master's in education candidate who once took a one-credit-hour workshop over the summer might realize a savings of $150 to $300 or more, if it could be applied to his or her program of study.

The use of previously earned credits must be checked out carefully, however. Graduate colleges and academic departments often have rules that limit their utility. First, there may be a time limit. Normally, all applicable course work must have been completed within a reasonable period of time prior to admission. This time period could vary, depending on the institution. In addition, there could be a limit on the number of hours that may be earned before admission. For example, at The University of Iowa, in a 32-semester-hour master's program, no more than 8 hours earned before admission may be applied to a program of study. This requirement is fairly typical.

I suggest that you resolve all questions about the admissibility of credits you may have already earned before you submit an application. The best way to check out such questions is to call the chairperson of the department or program offering the degree you are considering. That person can usually provide you with a definitive answer. If he or she either cannot answer your question in fairly short order or refer you to someone who can, you might want to consider whether or not you want to deal with such folks for the next few years.

You have probably noticed that I have left the formal part of checking on admissibility, the application itself, until last. This is the formal process in which your undergraduate grades, standardized test scores, and letters of recommendation will be checked out. It makes little sense to go to all of the time, trouble, and expense of preparing an application if you can rule out a program in advance. Furthermore, you won't want to bother the same people for letters of recommendation over and over again. Whereas it is good to move quickly once you know you have identified an appropriate institution, there is no reason to waste your time and money on superfluous applications. I will deal with the application process, in detail, later in this chapter.

▒ Reputation

How important to you is the reputation of the institution from which you want to obtain your degree? In the end, you have to weigh this factor against the others as you consider trade-offs.

Will the name of the school have a bearing on your career, or do you just need the degree? This will vary greatly according to your professional field and ambitions. If you are contemplating an MBA as a means of advancement in your company or in hopes of making an opportunistic career move, you should probably select the program with the best reputation, if you are admissible and can afford it. However, if you are a junior officer with plans to become a major and make the Air Force a career, the source of the degree is not nearly as important as the fact that you have earned it. If you are a teacher who plans to stay in the classroom and if you need the master's only to surpass salary barriers, any regionally accredited program should do. But if you want to become a principal or superintendent, reputation becomes more important.

It would be a good idea to find out just how important reputation is in practical terms. Ask your boss or the personnel office how your company regards the schools you are considering. If your employer will reimburse your tuition for a given university, that is a good sign. If you can do so discreetly, try to find out how other local employers feel. Ask your colleagues with advanced degrees how having graduated from given programs has helped or hurt them.

Do you have reason to believe that one school is as good as its reputation and another is as poor? Check it out carefully. The reference shelves in most libraries and comprehensive bookstores have all sorts of titles that deal with this issue. However, most are oriented to the mobile, youthful, full-time student who can travel virtually anywhere. In most cases, you will be comparing only two or three available schools. Although such sources are certainly worth a look, your time will be much better spent in asking people (a) who have reason to know something about the issue and (b) whose opinion you respect.

If two programs are available and one costs twice as much as the other, does the better name justify the greater expense? On the whole, I would be inclined to say no, unless the gap in reputations were extremely wide. On the other hand, if the program I perceived to have greater distinction cost only 50% more, I would seriously consider going with it, all other factors being equal. But of course, all other factors are never equal. This could be the toughest trade-off you will face.

Is the school's name important to you as a source of ego gratification? This question is not as trivial as it sounds. You certainly do not want to be ashamed of the school from which you will earn an advanced degree. But beyond that, reputation can matter. If you are active in business, an MBA from the most prestigious of your state's universities may serve you well. In addition, your fellow alums may become important contacts.

Schools market their reputations. The university in which I work is generally regarded to have the best graduate programs in the state in virtually all the curricular areas we offer. Those of us who work with programs designed for part-time students maximize our school's reputation in our promotional campaigns. Other than immediate geographic proximity, no factor is nearly as important in our recruiting.

▓ Comparative Costs

Graduate degrees are not cheap. Cost represents one of the major trade-off considerations. Virtually all other issues relate to funding in one way or another.

Evaluating costs is not always a matter of comparing tuition per credit hour. Graduate programs have varying credit-hour requirements. MBAs, for example, range from 32 to 60 semester hours, or the quarter-hour equivalent. Where a state university may have the lowest per-hour tuition, a nearby private institution with a higher tuition may be able to offer its program at a lower overall cost by requiring fewer credit hours. Should this be the case, you would then need to consider such factors as quality, reputation, content of the curriculum, and format.

There are other cost-related factors to consider. If one program would require you to take prerequisites as part of your program of study where another would not, the difference in costs might be significant. If the tuition and credit-hour requirements were close to the same at two universities but the location of one would involve considerable travel, this would become a financial consideration. Perhaps you took a course or two a few years ago. If one school would accept those credit hours but the other would not, this might change the financial picture.

Sometimes decision making can be simple. If you have access to only one program, your only option is to take it or leave it. If you work for a company that is bringing a program into your workplace and will pick up the cost of the program, it's a "no brainer." Not only will you be relieved of the cost entirely, you will not have to put up with the time and expense of a commute. And, more important, you will have the assurance that this program will benefit you within your company. There is yet another cost factor to consider. Although universities are always open and forthright about their tuition rate, they can be less revealing when it comes to fees. Many schools and programs have tried to cope with the rising costs of such things as computer labs and library serials by assessing fees, sometimes on a per-course basis, other times as sort of a surcharge for admission into a given program, such as the MBA. If these fees are collected as a per-hour surcharge, the part-timer actually ends up paying more than the full-time student.

Fees tend to become entrenched. And because many schools can raise fees without going to their trustees or governing boards, they tend to grow. Therefore, be sure to check out secondary and hidden costs when considering competing programs.

FORMATS FOR PART-TIME STUDY

Teaching formats designed specifically for the working, adult, part-time student started to emerge about a century ago, when many state universities and a few private schools, most notably the University of Chicago, made "extension" a part of their missions. The initial extension teaching formats were on-campus evening classes; off-campus classes (usually called extension courses), requiring faculty to travel to sites distant from campus; and correspondence study. From the beginning, evening courses drew enrollments from a variety of disciplinary areas, whereas off-campus courses primarily served teachers seeking professional development and advancement. Most universities used correspondence study mainly for undergraduate or even vocational course work but placed severe limits on its use at the graduate level or forbade it altogether. Whereas additional formats designed primarily for part-time students have developed since the 19th century, they all represent variations or descendants of these three schemes.

The range of available program formats may have a considerable impact on your decision. If two or more institutions in your area offer an appropriate program, the convenience of the formats becomes an issue. You might have to choose between classes offered in the evenings and classes offered during your workday. The latter would require considerable cooperation from your employer. You might live in such a remote area that only programs offered via distance education formats offer a real opportunity. Your schedule might be such that only programs offered asynchronously (not in real time) could work for you. Once again, note how all the trade-offs inevitably involve access and cost.

Unless your employer is offering courses at your work site, it is usually preferable to attend classes at night or on weekends or to find an asynchronous distance education format, rather than juggle your work schedule around classes. Despite the best possible intentions on your part and your employer's, regular absences during the work day will create strains among your peers.

The office in which I work is on a campus. We value advanced degrees and we depend on part-time students as our audience. Therefore, it is our policy to encourage our employees to seek degrees, both graduate and undergraduate. This is no hollow pronouncement. We pay the tuition for one course per semester. Even so, a few of our employees carefully watch the comings and goings of their class-bound colleagues. Resentment can occur even in an office with near-optimum conditions. In offices where education is not openly supported, conditions will likely be even worse. This is just human nature, of course; but for that reason, it is always with us.

Such a schedule will also disrupt your work and is apt to produce guilt on your part or at least hypersensitivity to the feelings of your co-workers. Despite your best efforts, it could put you behind schedule and on the defensive. And there will be times when you simply will not be able to get to a class because of an important meeting or a deadline. Furthermore, even the most understanding boss will sometimes find your schedule inconvenient.

Given all of these potential problems, it is usually preferable to go to school on your own time. This tends to keep your working relationships on an even keel and—just as important—to protect your privacy. Remember, however, that as bothersome as this issue can be, it is only one more factor in your decision. If you can only get the program you want—or even some of its classes—in the daytime, and if you can work it out with your employer, then do so. Just be prepared for petty annoyances and hurt feelings. You will survive, and so will your colleagues. Chapter 7 addresses this problem in detail.

As competition for the adult student has grown, and with the advancement of technology, North American universities have developed a variety of instructional formats to make their programs more accessible. As you consider the range of available programs, do not confuse instructional format with program quality. The conventional wisdom seems to be that residential, full-time instruction is the superior teaching mode and that all other formats must be measured against it. The further a delivery format varies from this model, according to this simplistic line of thinking, the less the quality of the educational experience. In educational terms, it simply is not so.

The college of education closest to your home probably offers a master's degree in instructional design and technology via the conventional daytime residential format. Perhaps it is also available wholly or partially through evening classes. George Washington University offers its Master of Arts in Educational Technology Leadership, through videotape and e-mail, to students anywhere in the country and overseas. Although there may be good reasons to take the program from your local university, perhaps cost or a greater level of comfort with the conventional classroom format, the quality of the program and the comparative reputations of the schools certainly would not put George Washington at a disadvantage. Remember, it's the institution, not the format.

Evening Courses

Evening classes are the old standard for extending access to part-time students. Hundreds of U.S. universities offer classes and programs, including graduate programs, at night. Night school is so entrenched in popular culture that we have highly recognizable stereotypes of students and teachers. I once did some research on how adult students are portrayed in popular films and fiction. Generally, they are either losers, who couldn't possibly succeed in "real" college, or virtuous overachievers who, despite juggling multiple roles, are on the fast track to success (Pittman, 1992). Actually, night school students, like other students, run the gamut from brilliance to incompetence, with most falling between the extremes.

Urban universities have institutionalized evening classes, often as a means of raising revenue. Evening students do not require the same level of service—they make little use of gyms, student unions, and the like—and they place no additional demands on the physical plant. Yet they pay the same tuition. And at most schools, over the course of a degree program, they will pay more. This is because most universities give full-time students a tremendous break on tuition. Once a full-time student hits an arbitrary number of credit hours per semester, the school caps the tuition. The student pays a flat rate, regardless of the number of hours for which he or she is enrolled. For example, if a university capped its tuition of $163 per semester hour at nine hours, a full-time student who took 12 hours in each of his or her first two semesters, then eight more to complete the program, would pay $4,238 over the course of a 32-hour master's degree. A part-time student taking one or two 3-hour courses per semester would pay $5,216, almost $1,000 more.

This is not to say that you should avoid institutions that are trying to make a buck on night courses. Most successful bargains are based on what diplomatic historians call "mutual interests," and what pop psychologists call "win-win" situations. If a program meets your specifications for accessibility, cost, quality, and reputation, it would not be smart to shy away just because the institution is benefiting financially from your enrollment. There are a couple of things you will want to check out, however.

Many evening programs have traditionally relied on adjunct faculty. These are instructors who are not full-time, tenure-track professors in the institution offering the classes. Sometimes, they are professors from other colleges. More often, they are practitioners in the field of study being taught. Like you, they come to class after a day's work. For example, professional accountants often teach business courses; school superintendents may teach education courses.

Such professors and instructors are by no means necessarily inferior. Many have the same degrees as full-time faculty. Often, their practical experience provides insights that full-time professors could not duplicate. They can add a great deal to a program, especially one designed for working professionals. However, adjuncts normally do not have the research experience of professors, with the cutting-edge knowledge it generates. They do not influence the curriculum of a program, share its philosophical orientation, or participate in its administration. As a general rule of thumb, a limited use of adjuncts is fine, even desirable. However, in most cases, I would suggest avoiding programs that rely on them for the bulk of instruction.

In evaluating an evening program, you should also consider the school's commitment to serving you. You probably will not want to make use of the full range of services and facilities available to daytime students, but what about those that are important to you? Will the library be open during hours in which you can use it? If you need computer access or support, will it be available? Will you qualify for student rates for athletic and theater tickets? Although answers to questions like these are not difficult to obtain from the institution, your best bet is to ask other part-time students. Besides getting the facts, you can get a feel for the school's attitude toward students like yourself.

▓ Intensive Weekends

Long hours of class scheduled on weekends provide another campus-based format for part-time students. At most institutions, the class schedule provides the same number of contact hours per term as conventional on-campus courses. This format extends the range of an institution's graduate programs, because many—if not most—students live at a distance from the campus. Typically, they drive in on Friday afternoon or evening, attend classes through Saturday evening or Sunday morning, then drive home.

Education colleges have long offered this format at both the doctoral and master's levels. The one at The University of Iowa is designed to allow students to take two courses per term. The Graduate School of Library and Information Science at the University of Illinois offers an interesting variant. In its "Fridays Only" program, working librarians who commute long distance can earn the MS in Library and Information Science in approximately five semesters.

Colleges of business frequently use variations of this intensive weekend format to offer "executive" MBA programs. The following description of its executive MBA class schedule is from the recruiting brochure of a Big Ten university's school of management:

> The program begins with a five-day Residency Week in mid-August and ends 21 months later with graduation in May of the second year.
> Residency Week provides an intense introduction to the Executive MBA program. Participants stay at a downtown hotel, attend classes during the day, join in group activities and study sessions in the evening, and interact extensively with peers and professors. For the remainder of the academic year, classes meet one day per week— alternately on Fridays or Saturdays—[on campus]. Following a three-

month summer break, the second year also begins with Residency Week.

I have quoted at length because this provides an excellent example of a program designed to serve a highly selective audience. Notice that it is conducted in strict cohort style. Each student takes exactly the same courses. Degree programs offered through intensive weekend schedules and their variations can be grueling, but they have worked well for many people.

Off-Campus Courses

Off-campus classes date back to the founding of the land grant colleges in the late 19th and early 20th centuries. The first off-campus graduate programs came several decades later, mainly in the degree field of education. Now, earning a graduate degree—most commonly the professional master's—at sites removed from university campuses is a widespread practice. Traditionally, universities have staffed these programs by sending their professors to teach, usually on a one-night-per-week basis, or by heavy use of adjunct faculty, or both.

For the usual reasons of access, most off-campus programs are offered in the evening. However, there are exceptions, mainly when courses are offered in the workplace under corporate sponsorship. Firms such as Boeing and Rockwell International have long taken advantage of this model to provide graduate classes to their employees.

Sites for off-campus graduate course programming vary widely. Many current colleges and universities actually began as branch campuses or "extension centers," offering evening courses to working adults. Several universities in Georgia's Regents System, for example, got their start this way. Sometimes, degree programs are offered by several institutions at consortial graduate centers, such as the Quad Cities Graduate Study Center, in Rock Island, Illinois, and the Tri-State Graduate Center, in Sioux City, Iowa. Universities often lease space from community colleges or private four-year colleges so that they can have the advantages of collegiate support facilities and services, such as standard classrooms and computer labs in which to offer their graduate programs. Beyond that, universities sometimes work out course-by-course arrangements with high schools, churches, and corporate training facilities.

In evaluating graduate programs at off-campus sites, consider the same issues as you would for evening classes. Is the program taught by the actual faculty or by adjuncts barely connected to the university? What kind of library and computer support access is provided? How does the curriculum suit you? Is the cost fair and affordable? Another factor to consider is whether or not the entire degree program is available at the off-campus site. Sometimes, a program requires students to come to campus, either during a specified term— such as the summer between two years of a cohort program—or for a minimum number of credit hours. If this is the case, will you be able and willing to rearrange your work and family life to meet this requirement?

The Council of Graduate Schools has published a set of guidelines for off-campus programs, designed to help universities set and maintain programmatic standards. You should find these guidelines helpful as you evaluate programs, whether offered at off-campus sites or via distance education media. This Academic Guidelines Policy Statement is included in Appendix B.

Military Bases

A graduate degree is more than an asset to young officers who wish to make a career of the military. In fact, it has become a de facto requirement for promotion beyond the first three officer grades. For this reason, graduate programs are offered on base at many U.S. military installations around the world. Officers, enlisted personnel, and even dependents can use these highly convenient facilities.

Some schools, notably Central Michigan University and Webster University in St. Louis, have created specialized formats through which to provide degrees at such sites. Central Michigan offers a Master of Science in Administration degree, with standardized core courses and a modest range of concentration areas, at more than 35 sites, the majority of which are located on military installations. A student can take half the program at one base, be transferred thousands of miles away, and then take the remaining courses and graduate.

In addition to the availability of such flexible programs, there are other factors favorable to military officers taking degrees on a part-time basis. It is not uncommon for the military to station an officer in a given location for the specific purpose of taking course work. Also, at least since the end of the Cold War, there has been a tendency for the services to lengthen the duration of tours. That is, an officer will typically serve for several years at a given duty station, providing more time in which to pursue a complete degree program.

▓ "Suitcase" or Cluster Colleges

Cluster programs, for the lack of a better name, combine the intensive weekend and off-campus formats. Nova Southeastern University, located in Ft. Lauderdale, Florida, developed this format in the early 1970s. A "national" faculty of adjunct professors, along with full-time professors based on the home campus, flew to "clusters," or cohorts, of students located throughout the country. The students were working educators who enrolled in the National EdD Program for Educational Leaders. Nova then extended this format to deliver five additional doctoral and four master's programs. Initially controversial, Nova persisted, earned regional accreditation, and to date has graduated more than 10,000 part-time students through its cluster format (Goldman, 1996).

▓ Distance Education

For more than a century, colleges and universities have used distance education as a means of serving part-time students. The University of Chicago institutionalized distance education by making correspondence study a part of its organic structure at its founding in 1892. However, it became a significant course delivery format mainly at the undergraduate level. Graduate colleges resisted it as something radical, educationally suspect. The people who ran collegiate correspondence programs were unable to overcome the popular image of sleaziness created by some of the more flamboyant, and even fraudulent, proprietary correspondence schools. Vestiges of this bias remain, particularly in some graduate colleges, where innovation is resisted reflexively.

Beginning in the early 1970s, however, the tide began to turn. Some of the finest engineering colleges in the country, including the Massachusetts Institute of Technology and Stanford University, began to use videotape to deliver course work and professional master's degrees to working engineers at their work sites.

As new media have become available, more and more schools have begun to offer course work and degrees, at all levels, to working adult students. It is now possible to earn degrees from such solid institutions as George Washington University, Colorado State University, Ball State

University, and—soon—The New School for Social Research, from
anywhere in the nation. Chapter 3 will examine the delivery of
graduate programs to part-time students through the various media of
distance education. For now, it is sufficient to note that distance
education delivery formats are quickly and drastically increasing the
range of available options for part-time graduate study.

FACING THE GATEKEEPER:
THE ADMISSIONS PROCESS

To gain admission to the program of your choice, you will probably
have to make take the Graduate Record Examination (GRE) or the
Graduate Management Admission Test (GMAT). Carefully study the
application materials for details and specific instructions, then submit
an application, solicit about three letters of recommendation, and
forward all your transcripts to the university office that handles
graduate admissions. Not all graduate programs require all of these
steps.

Your application materials will probably circulate through several
university offices—the graduate college, the academic college, the
department offering the program, and perhaps others. The larger the
university, the greater the certainty of overlapping jurisdictions. However, the instructions on the application form will provide the address
of the office that serves as the starting point.

Entrance Exams

If you are seriously considering graduate school, plan to take the
GRE or the GMAT as soon as possible. In many schools, admissions
committees meet infrequently. They, like many other parts of the
higher education bureaucracy, set their schedules to match the academic year rhythms of full-time students. If you miss an admissions
date because you did not have your test scores in, your admission could
be delayed by as long as 6 months.

If you should miss an admissions deadline for this reason, most
schools will allow you to take courses in a preadmission status, but a
few will not. Even those that do allow this practice may have a strict
limit, perhaps six or eight credit hours. The only reason for delaying
admissions tests might be the expense. At last notice, the GRE's

General Test cost $64 in the United States and $89 elsewhere, with subject tests, if necessary, offered at the same rate. Again, however, if you are serious about graduate school, it is probably a good move to take at least the GRE General Test. You may also need subject tests for some schools. If so, the information will be available in the school's catalog and with the application materials.

Taking the test early may give you another advantage. If you should do badly, you might have time to repeat it before the next admissions deadline. And if you do well, it will be one less step in completing your application when the time comes.

It is possible to minimize the scheduling problem, at least for the GRE General Test, by taking it via computer. Whereas the conventional pencil-and-paper test is administered only on three fixed dates per year, you may take it via computer at virtually any time at more than 225 test centers in the United States and a handful outside the country. The computer option is more expensive, at $96 in the United States and $120 elsewhere, and subject area tests are not yet available.

Should you take a course to prepare for the GRE or GMAT? There is no easy answer. On the one hand, part-time students get into graduate programs every day, most with no special preparation. On the other hand, it may have been a long time since you have been in a classroom or have even taken a test. Thus, anxiety, as well as rusty math and vocabulary skills, may be a problem. Research on the performance of older people who take the GRE is fairly encouraging. Stricker and Rock (1987) found that although scores on the quantitative and analytical sections of the tests did decline with age, the loss was not precipitous. More important, age seemed to have no impact at all on scores on the verbal section of the test. Some programs are oriented to part-time adult students and will cut them some slack on test scores, but I would not count on it.

If you decide to take a review course of some sort, it will probably help you. At the very least, it should help get you back into a test-taking frame of mind and make the actual testing experience less intimidating.

Iowa's school kids have always been at or near the very top in terms of standardized test scores, from grade school through the SATs and ACTs. Is this because Iowa kids are smarter than children in the rest of the country? Although those of us who live here would like to think so, we really know better. Developing standardized tests is an Iowa industry. Many tests used across the country are tried out extensively on our children, who "fill in the bubbles" year after year. As a result, Iowa kids become highly test-wise. They learn how to take standardized tests and are not intimidated by them. As a result, they score well.

A review course, if it does nothing else, could help you overcome the normal anxiety of the test situation. More than likely, just solving some test problems ahead of time will help your performance. Several review courses and manuals are listed in Appendix C. If you do nothing else, you can order a free copy of the *General Test Descriptive Booklet* for the GRE. It contains sample questions, suggested strategies, and a practice test. This booklet is available from Graduate Record Examinations at the address given in Appendix C.

Completing the Application

It would seem to go without saying that anyone applying for graduate school must fill out the application neatly, completely, and in accordance with all instructions. However, it certainly doesn't always happen that way. I have occasionally served on my teaching department's admissions committee and have also seen many applications for programs that my administrative department (continuing education) has facilitated. All too often, they are sloppy and incomplete. Sometimes, it almost seems as if the candidate is applying for some program other than ours. Although an outstanding candidate can survive this kind of faux pas, a marginal one might not.

When you receive application materials, immediately make several copies of the application form. Use one or more of them as worksheets. As you provide the specified information, recheck dates, addresses, and phone numbers. For example, it is not uncommon for a candidate to list a former employer, then give an erroneous address or give the wrong dates of attendance at another college or university.

After checking out your worksheet thoroughly, fill out the actual application. Or better yet, have a professional do it for you. Many of us are no longer competent working at typewriters, which are necessary for filling out forms. It would be well worth the small investment to pay a professional secretary to do this for you, if you know one. They are among the few people still capable of doing this kind of work.

Once you have assembled your neatly completed application and all the specified attachments, photocopy everything. Although it is unusual for items to get lost in the U.S. mail, on rare occasions, parts of them may disappear in their travels between university offices. Besides, it is good to keep a record. Most application forms call for much of the same information. Your first application can save you a lot of work on the second or third.

For many—if not most—programs, the application form will ask you to write an essay on your motives and expectations in attending graduate school. At The University of Iowa, this essay is called a "Statement of Purpose." Do not blow off this exercise. It is a critical element of the application process, particularly for students who have been out of school for several years. Your GRE scores, your undergraduate grade point average, and any grades for earlier graduate work are now beyond your control; you can do nothing to improve them. This essay is the one element of your application you can control.

Perhaps you had a mediocre undergraduate record; many of us did. The application essay will give you a chance to partially rehabilitate your academic reputation. If you have been teaching successfully for many years and have earned commendations and awards, say so. If you are responsible for the work of 200 sailors at your current duty station, this says something about your administrative experience and ability. Few of us are the same people we were 10, or even 5, years ago. Use this essay to tell the admissions committee who you are now.

Describe how this degree program will help you meet your professional goals. Although it is certainly acceptable to say that you need the degree as a credential to advance your career, do not stop at that. Try to show some understanding of how the course work can help in your professional growth. If possible, use specific examples, citing some of the individual courses. Then turn the coin over. Describe how your presence will benefit the program. How will the insights you have gained in your career be instructive to your fellow students and perhaps even to the faculty? If you have any demonstrated research experience, or currently perform research, or use research results in the course of doing your job, be sure to say so.

As you write your essay, do not worry about eloquence. Strive for clear, straightforward prose and a businesslike tone. Make sure you have made no grammatical or typographical errors. Have someone you know to be a good editor read it to look for any errors you might have missed and to help you strengthen your argument. Then, and only then, transfer your essay to the application form, or attach it, as directed.

Although there are no guarantees, a strong application essay can help an admissions committee concentrate on your seriousness of purpose, current capabilities, and potential, rather than on a 10-year-old undergraduate record or less-than-optimum test scores.

▓ Letters of Recommendation

Letters of recommendation can be a real problem for someone who has been out of school for several years. This is a part of the application process that many institutions need to reconsider. However, for now, most graduate school application packages specify letters of recommendation, usually three.

If there is a professor in your past with whom you had a particularly positive experience, especially if you have kept in touch, try that person. If you have taken or are taking some graduate course work in a preadmission status, ask that professor (or those professors) for a letter. Be sure to explain the situation to them. And if you are currently in such a class or classes, do your absolute best. The opinion of these professors will carry a great deal of weight with the admissions committee, because their observations will be contemporaneous.

Your employer or supervisor should be one of your references. If you work in an educational institution, such as a school district or a community college, so much the better. This person, like those cited earlier, should be able to speak to your *potential* as a student. After all, potential is really what the admissions committee is looking for.

It is always a good idea to give a copy of your resume to anyone you ask to write a letter of recommendation. It refreshes their memories and helps them fill in the gaps in time. Besides, if you have not revised your resume, or curriculum vitae, recently, it is time to do so. Then, keep it current. As an actual or potential graduate student, you will often need it to attach to forms of all sorts, including applications for admission or funding. And perhaps you will want to use it as you apply for new positions as you near completion of your graduate degree.

CONCLUSION

If you decide that you want to go to graduate school, and if you are accepted by more than one program, it will be time to carefully consider all of the trade-offs mentioned in this chapter. You will have to determine the comparative advantages of accessibility and cost, as well as quality, support services, and reputation. No available options will be without both advantages and disadvantages. Make the trade-offs, then don't look back.

REFERENCES

Goldman, R. (1996). Nova Southeastern University: Pioneering efforts in distance education. *Adult Assessment Forum, 6,* 6-8.

McCook, D., & Moen, W. E. (1992). Patterns of program selection: Ranked factors in the choice of a master's degree program in library and information studies. *Journal of Education for Library and Information Science, 33*(3), 212-225.

Pittman, V. (1992). Outsiders in academe: Night school in American fiction. *The Journal of Continuing Higher Education, 40,* 8-13.

Stricker, L. J., & Rock, D. A. (1987). Factor structure of the GRE General Test in young and middle adulthood. *Developmental Psychology, 23*(4), 526-536.

3

GRADUATE STUDY
AT A DISTANCE

I have been a stranger in a strange land.
—Exodus 2:22

Distance education is currently enjoying a great boom at all levels in U.S. education, including—finally—graduate education. The popular press is selling it as a new concept, but it has been part of the U.S. collegiate scene—albeit a minor part—since the 19th century. After some fitful experimentation with in absentia instruction in the 1870s and 1880s, founding president William Rainey Harper made a correspondence study department an integral part of the University of Chicago in 1892, thereby establishing its presence and legitimacy in postsecondary education. Other distance education formats began to appear as early as the 1920s, with instructional radio. Since then, colleges and universities have experimented with a number of distance education formats, adopting some and rejecting others.

The acceptance of distance education's legitimacy has come most slowly at the graduate level. Several explanations for this reluctance come to mind. First, and I think most important, are the natural conservatism and elitism of universities. Change comes slowly, and it comes hard, especially at the graduate level. As one wag joked, "It's harder to change a university than to move a cemetery, although the activities are similar."

Furthermore, graduate study has traditionally been the province of the intellectual elite, an activity for the select few. Distance education is based on a belief in extending access to education. Therefore, distance education at the graduate level has provided a point of conflict between two ideological tendencies—elitism and a commitment to democracy—within the U.S. university. The fact that these tendencies are essentially incompatible does not prevent either individuals or institutions from simultaneously embracing both.

Historically, distance education's most avid proponents must share responsibility for its slow and conditional acceptance. With each new delivery medium—from radio through computers—promoters have oversold its potential, promising one educational revolution after another. Their overblown promises of what Thomas Russell (1996) called "the panacea du jour" (p. 22) have clashed with the innate conservatism of graduate education. With each revolution that did not happen, the fervent advocates of the various instructional formats not only diminished their own credibility, they damaged the credibility of distance delivery of courses and programs in general.

In recent years, however, the increased sophistication of distance education media, the growth of competition for graduate students—particularly those who pay their own tuition—and the ascendance of a generation of professors who grew up with telecommunications have finally begun to erode traditional reservations. Even highly traditional graduate colleges at premier universities have begun to offer selected programs via distance education.

According to Craig Swenson (1995), university faculty members have two primary expectations of graduate—as opposed to under-graduate—study. First, they expect it to be more interactive in nature, with "debate and dialogue . . . expected to play a greater role" (p. 51). Second, the faculty expect greater independence on the part of graduate students. Although both points are valid, the latter contains a certain irony. Correspondence study, more than any other methodology, has demanded independence of the student. The traditional lecture hall method, with its dependence on the lecture and the direction of the instructor, requires very little. Yet, the former has traditionally been anathema in graduate colleges, and the latter, a matter of course. As newer technologies make it easier to replicate the lecture hall, professors are finding distance education increasingly credible.

Delivering graduate programs via distance education formats can provide distinct advantages to not only students but universities whose missions include serving professional audiences. Colleges of education, for example, have long struggled with providing graduate work to specialized—but geographically scattered—audiences, such as school librarians or special-education teachers. Traditionally, the most common format they have used has been off-campus or extension classes, to which professors either drove or were flown.

But in many areas, it has been difficult, if not impossible, to find critical mass, that is, enough students at a given site that could justify the time and expense of putting a professor on the road. Teachers either had to move to a campus in the summer or do without the courses their employers demanded for advancement. Other professional schools, notably engineering, have found the practice of sending professors to off-campus sites a serious drain on research time. In both these cases and in others, graduate programs have either been able to increase their efficiency in dealing with old audiences or extend access to new audiences through the use of distance education.

If you should consider a program delivered via distance education, keep in mind that "it's the institution." Do not confuse quality with format. Course delivery systems do not determine educational quality; professors and institutions do.

Hundreds of empirical research studies comparing various teaching formats—classroom, television, correspondence, computer-assisted learning, and others—have reported the same conclusion, that format has no influence on learning outcomes. Thomas Russell, a professor at North Carolina State University, has been collecting studies of comparative outcomes between courses conducted in a conventional manner and via distance education delivery formats, and between courses delivered via different distance education formats, for several years. His most recent compilation lists 214 comparative studies with essentially the same finding: no significant difference (Russell, 1995). His work reinforces the work of Clark (1983), a decade earlier, which concluded,

> The best current evidence is that media are mere vehicles that deliver instruction but do not influence achievement any more than the truck

that delivers our groceries causes changes in nutrition . . . only the content of the vehicle can influence achievement. (p. 445)

The finding that modes of instruction have no measurable effect on outcomes has become a cliché in educational research. In fact, this finding is now considered so predictable, and indeed so trite, that the College of Education at Penn State no longer allows doctoral research along these lines. There is nothing left to prove.

On the other hand, do not allow yourself to be overly impressed with promoters of the various media who might try to impress you with the glitz of high-tech instruction. Distance education, when delivered by a good institution, is neither cheap, easy, nor superior to the conventional product in any way except accessibility. Although you should not be deterred by academic snobbery, be skeptical of the hucksters—and there are some out there—who will try to tell you the medium is the message. Only the message is the message.

Degrees awarded for study via distance education media from state universities and prestigious private institutions should present no problems in terms of recognition in your profession's marketplace. A master's in engineering from Stanford or the University of Illinois will be received as such, whether you should take it on campus or at your workplace, mainly via videotape. The fact that many of the country's largest engineering and manufacturing firms pay to have such programs delivered in-house attests to their credibility. Problems with credibility, if there should be any, would be more likely in the case of institutions that offer only distance instruction. And even here, there are some important exceptions. In some specialized areas, distance-education-oriented institutions enjoy excellent reputations.

Obtaining a master's, especially a professional master's, partially or entirely through distance education is becoming more and more common. Increasingly, universities are relaxing or even waiving residency requirements. At the doctoral level, however, this is a much slower process. Residency and full-time, or close to full-time, study remain part of the dominant instructional model. But even here, things are beginning to change. In *How to Earn an Advanced Degree Without Going to Graduate School*, James Duffy (1994) lists 11 regionally accredited institutions that offer doctoral degrees via distance education, most in the fields of education or the human sciences. All but one require some on-campus visits, which range from 1 day to several months.

A recent addition to the field, which has debuted since Duffy's survey, is the doctorate in educational leadership and higher education from the University of Nebraska-Lincoln (UNL). As UNL describes the methodology, it consists of "self-paced courses conducted through interactive computer-based communication and journaling methodologies . . . offered via Lotus Notes Distributed Education." Lotus Notes is a form of "groupware" through which students can communicate with each other, as well as with the professor, on a regular but asynchronous basis. Although there are still fairly strict residency requirements—either two summer sessions or two consecutive semesters—this is a highly innovative and unusually accessible doctoral program. I feel certain that it will be imitated and, eventually, residency requirements will be relaxed. However, I also believe that as a practical matter, doctoral study through distance education, like any other kind of part-time program, will continue to be available primarily in education or human services. As with any kind of part-time program, demand regional accreditation at a minimum.

ACCEPTANCE OF DEGREES THROUGH DISTANCE EDUCATION

Distance education has a number of features that you may find attractive. For example, you might live and work in a place in which there are no accessible programs in your academic area. Or perhaps a distance education program would allow you to step up a notch in class, offering an opportunity to earn a degree from a nationally known university instead of one with a local or regional reputation. Depending again on location, the distance education program might offer a less costly way of working toward your goal. However, as unfair as this might be, it is possible that skepticism about graduate study via these methods might cause employers, or others, to question the value of your degree. Although this should not be a problem in the case of nationally known universities, it could be with lesser-known schools.

You must ask yourself as you consider each program whether it will do what you want it to do. Will it assist you in learning the skills and content you need to master? Will it serve as the credential you need for career purposes? This, of course, is far from an exact science. First, ask colleagues where you work and elsewhere. Perhaps, some of them either have taken degrees this way or had reason to decide against doing so. Ask your managers or supervisors. Will your employer either pay the tuition or reimburse you? In some situations, this is irrelevant. Few school systems, for example, assist their teachers with tuition costs. However, if your company supports tuition for some programs and not for others, it is sending a clear message. If a license is involved, check with the appropriate agency in your state.

Last, do not discount your gut feelings. You will expend considerable time, energy, and money earning a graduate degree. If you are worried that you may regret your choice of programs, you need to rethink the entire matter. Consider the pros and cons, the trade-offs that I have mentioned so frequently. After doing so, if you have reservations, pay attention to them.

DISTANCE EDUCATION METHODOLOGIES

The media and formats used in collegiate distance education vary so greatly that generalizations are difficult. However, despite their considerable differences, all distance instructional formats fall into one of two modes, synchronous or asynchronous. Synchronous formats are those that operate in so-called real time. Professors and all students meet for class at the same time, but not—of course—in the same place. In courses offered asynchronously, interaction between professors and students and among students—if there is any—is delayed or deferred. There are no class meetings per se. Within each general mode, there are numerous formats. There are also formats that mix synchronous and asynchronous elements. And especially at the graduate level, it is not uncommon to require at least a modicum of conventional resident classroom attendance.

As a general rule, the geographic "footprints" of programs operated asynchronously are much larger than those of synchronous, or real-time, programs. Also as a rule, programs that use synchronous instruction operate at a more controlled pace. But within these rules of thumb, universities and other distance education institutions have devised dozens of ways of serving students at a distance from their campuses.

▓   Correspondence, or "Independent," Study

Correspondence study is the oldest form of distance education. Some educators date it back to St. Paul's epistles in the New Testament. It has been a fixture in U.S. postsecondary education since 1892, when as we saw earlier, the University of Chicago opened with a home-study department in its Division of Extension. Now, more often than not, this format is called "independent study." University correspondence directors first adopted this term to stress the students' solitary learning experience and the fact that within limits, they controlled the pace of instruction. Also, these directors hoped to disassociate their product from the flashy and misleading advertising, shabby reputations, and frequent scandals associated with many proprietary, or commercial, correspondence schools. Do not, by the way, confuse independent study in this context with the individualized reading courses or projects set up on a one-professor, one-student basis.

U.S. universities have most often used correspondence study as a means of "filling in." Most students who have used it have taken only one or two courses, mainly to solve scheduling problems or cover a period of forced dislocation. Generally, universities have maintained a strict limit on the number of correspondence course credits a student could apply to a degree program, and even then, they almost always limited this practice to undergraduates. During the 1970s, a number of universities developed external degrees. In these programs, students could apply large numbers of correspondence credits to an under-graduate degree.

University graduate schools traditionally have been slow to accept correspondence study or have resisted it altogether. In fact, attitudes have run from adamant opposition to grudging acceptance. The University of Iowa fits into the latter category. A student may take up to 9 hours out of a 32-hour master's program through correspondence study. And for a major research university, that is fairly daring.

For graduate degree work, the independent-study method is most often used in highly specialized programs, with a national or interna-tional audience. The College for Financial Planning, a unit of the National Endowment for Financial Education, offers the Master of Science degree, with a concentration in personal financial planning, entirely through correspondence study. Both the institution and the degree, accredited through the North Central Association, enjoy superb reputations within the field of financial planning. In my experience with graduate education, I have found the level of student satisfaction with this program unparalleled. In fact, a surprising number of the students in this program already have advanced degrees, mainly in business or law.

The Master of Public Health programs at the Medical College of Wisconsin serve a national audience. They accept only practicing physicians as students and are conducted exclusively through independent study, except for an initial one-day orientation session on campus (although students are strongly encouraged to return for graduation). The University of Minnesota's School of Public Health offers similar programs but with the addition of regional preceptors with whom students hold monthly meetings to review their work. These schools and universities have found independent study the optimum format, given their highly motivated student populations, national recruiting areas, and specialized curricula.

Videotape-Based Courses

The use of videotape to extend graduate degree programs began in 1967, when Colorado State University established an engineering program, using the new 1-inch tape format (Davis, 1995). Colleges of Engineering from other leading institutions—including Stanford, the Massachusetts Institute of Technology, and Georgia Tech—soon adopted this methodology as a means of making master's-level degree work available to professional engineers, most frequently at their places of work.

The initial means of using this medium consisted of videotaping on-campus classes, including student comments, then sending the tapes to business and industrial sites normally in the same community, or at least the same state, where students viewed them, usually in small groups. The tapes could then be sent to one or more additional sites in the same area. All students in a course would normally view each class within a week of the day it was given on campus. Professors supplemented the tapes with telephone "office hours," and in some cases with occasional on-site visits. As videotape duplication became easier and cheaper, tapes could be sent to all off-campus sites and even individual students. Now, both live and taped classes are frequently uplinked to a satellite, then downlinked at sites—often factories—where students can either watch them live or record them for viewing at a convenient time. E-mail and computer simulations now supplement the telephone in providing interaction.

From the beginning, the emphasis of this format has been instruction and communication, not high production value. It has picked up the nickname of the "hairy forearm school of distance education," because so much of what the tape shows is an instructor writing on a chalkboard. This, of course, replicates what on-campus students see in some graduate engineering classes. This medium has thrived because it is aimed at a highly motivated, practically oriented, professional audience that enjoys strong support from its employers.

This basic, locally produced, videotape instruction model has inspired a number of variations. Engineering colleges pioneered it; now, other disciplines use it. Originally, its distribution was limited geographically. Now such courses are available nationally, by satellite delivery, cable systems, and rapid courier services.

Engineering students, in particular, enjoy several options, especially if they have employer support. Many have access to videotape-based programs through universities in their states. In addition, over 40 of the best engineering colleges in the country provide courses to a consortial institution, National Technological University (NTU), which offers seven master's programs and is accredited by the North Central Association. And like many of its member engineering colleges, NTU has gained the respect of corporate and industrial interests.

Students in many parts of the country have the option of pursuing engineering or technical degrees in their workplaces from their state universities, universities in other states, or NTU. For example, Alcoa has contracts with both the Virginia Consortium and the National Technological University to deliver classes to a dozen of its installations around the country. Thus, Alcoa employees can take an identical curriculum, even though they are scattered around the country and even though there might be only one or two participating employees in some plants.

The videotape-based format and its descendants work according to the pace of a semester system but are still essentially asynchronous in nature. The students view the tapes and interact with the professors according to their own schedules. Although NTU makes courses available in real time via satellite with audio return, most engineers prefer the asynchronous format. According to NTU's president, three quarters of its students report that because of their schedules, they prefer viewing videotapes to synchronous attendance (Davis, 1995).

Although engineering colleges developed videotape-based graduate courses and still account for the bulk of enrollments via that medium, other programs are available. For example, in addition to its engineering programs, Colorado State University offers master's programs in statistics, vocational education, and computer science, as well as the MBA. George Washington University's Master's in Educational Technology Leadership, mentioned in Chapter 2, also uses a variation of this format.

▓ Interactive Television

Interactive television is by far the dominant synchronous mode of distance education. It is a descendant of audioconferencing, a format that saw limited use in graduate education. Interactive television can take several forms. It can be delivered by satellite, compressed video (delivered via telephone lines), point-to-point microwave relay, extremely low-power broadcast television, and, by far the best variant, fiber-optic networks. Types of interaction vary. Some systems are one-way video or two-way audio, whereas others offer two-way video as well as audio.

Most interactive television programs are offered over networks that serve limited areas, due to either technological limitations of the systems or their costs and complexities. Some networks have the capacity to serve entire states, but most are a good deal less ambitious. Because of the nature of the technology, universities offer classes at fixed sites rather than to students in their homes, as is often the case with asynchronous instruction.

It is technologically possible to serve extremely large areas through satellite delivery, but the very high cost—in the neighborhood of $600 per hour for transmission alone—curtails such applications. As I noted earlier, NTU uses satellite delivery for its programs, although most students tape the downlinked sessions. Ball State University uses satellite delivery to reach 65 sites in Indiana, Kentucky, and New Jersey with an MBA program accredited by the AACSB.

Local or statewide networks offer a number of advantages. They make it feasible to serve small, scattered populations with synchronous instruction. A university could not afford to send a professor to a location 200 miles away to offer a special-education degree program to three people. However, if it can add those three people to three or four people in six or seven additional sites, the task becomes feasible.

It is this ability to form a critical mass from scattered students located at considerable distances from universities and from each other that makes interactive television systems so well suited to graduate work.

As noted earlier, I am currently teaching in a higher education program whose students are mainly community college employees. Because the state of Iowa built a statewide fiber-optic system, the Iowa Communications Network, we are able to offer this program to about 25 students in seven separate sites, from Council Bluffs in the west to the Quad Cities in the east.

Dozens of universities are using such systems to deliver real-time programs in disciplines ranging from agriculture and business to nursing and social work, in towns that have never before had access to graduate work. Perhaps equally important is the apparent credibility of this method. Universities that previously had shown either no interest in distance education or had disdained it altogether have begun to take advantage of this teaching format to extend programs to off-campus audiences.

Interactive television, although definitely a synchronous format, has a valuable asynchronous feature. In most programs, all classes are videotaped. The primary reason for taping classes is to provide a backup in case of technical problems at any of the sites. If a site suddenly goes "down," the students there can see the class belatedly at home or in a learning site. However, most often, students who have had to miss a class may request a tape. We have found that working professionals often have to miss occasional classes. They may suddenly be sent to another city to take care of a crisis, a meeting may run late, or they may have to entertain a visiting fireman. In the context of professional work, these are not trivial excuses. Professors generally understand such situations. Having a backup system works to everyone's benefit.

▦ Online Education

Computer-assisted education has been around since 1960, when the Control Data Corporation and the University of Illinois introduced PLATO, the first programmed-learning system. But widely accessible, college-level, computer-based distance education has only come of age in the 1990s. Now, "online" education, based on the capabilities and resources of the Internet, is making a huge impact on higher education. Currently, the governors of 13 western states are prompting the development of a Western Governors University (WGU). This institution, according to its charge, will have little or no physical plant but will offer graduate and undergraduate programs.

Whatever the fate of the WGU, online, Internet-based teaching formats are already with us, many well established and respected. Students from anywhere in the country can enroll in a Master of Science in Industrial Technology from East Carolina University, offered entirely online. Purdue University's Krannert Graduate School of Management intersperses six 2-week residential sessions with online instruction to offer its prestigious, AACSB-accredited Master of Science in Management nationwide. Many other universities now have programs either under way or in development.

In terms of the innovative use of the technology, the most impressive program with which I am familiar is the MBA program offered by the University of Phoenix (UOP) Online. This program, based in San Francisco's financial district and accredited by the North Central Association, forms classes as students enroll. When the last person in a specified class section—usually 12 or 13 people—enrolls, the course begins. A student works with his or her classmates, who are scattered all over the country, using the case-study method and reporting to the professor at least once a week. The student-teacher and student-student interaction is extensive, a fact that UOP can prove because it archives all computer communication.

Like the other major categories of distance education, computer-assisted, or online, teaching is offered in a number of variations. It is largely asynchronous but usually paced. In some cases, it is much like correspondence study, only much faster. In other cases, students work on joint projects with teams of classmates scattered over large geographic areas. Like correspondence study, it has the largest possible footprint available in distance education. Students can participate from anywhere, provided they can secure the requisite equipment and telecommunications services. As with any other distance education format, a program's reputation largely rests on that of the institution offering it.

INTERNATIONAL UNIVERSITIES

Online education's large footprint makes it not only feasible but fairly simple to earn credits from a school in one country while living in another. Some of the most sophisticated work in distance education is being delivered by universities located outside the United States but accessible within. Edinburgh Business School of Heriot-Watt University, in Scotland, claims that more than 10,000 students from around the world have enrolled in its MBA by Distance Learning program since 1970. Of its class that entered in 1996, the largest group (20%) of students are from the United States and Canada combined followed closely by Hong Kong, and then Singapore. North American students access Heriot-Watt via America Online.

Unlike Heriot-Watt, which maintains a conventional campus in addition to its online program, Athabasca University, in Alberta, is strictly a distance education institution. It, too, offers the MBA, using Lotus Notes group software, backed up with computer access to a library of more than 100,000 serial articles. Appropriately enough, Athabasca, which is to a large degree modeled after the British Open University, also offers a Master of Distance Education entirely by distance delivery.

Universities that offer programs internationally via distance education offer both advantages and disadvantages. Often, they are highly innovative. Unlike many universities in the United States, which essentially take a defensive position, they do not aspire simply to provide the closest possible imitation of a conventional face-to-face classroom. Instead, they aggressively try to develop the unique advantages of the various media of delivery. Some enjoy considerable support from their governments. Furthermore, like U.S. institutions that provide distance education only, they make the part-time student their target audience, not an afterthought. Therefore, many of the ordinary hurdles of conventional graduate school simply do not apply.

There are also disadvantages to consider. Such institutions are not well known in the United States. And, of course, they are not regionally accredited. Although they are generally accredited or licensed by the governments of the countries in which they are located, such credentials are difficult to evaluate for you or for your employer. Their instruction, of necessity, is asynchronous and independent. If you are not psychologically prepared for the rigor and considerable self-discipline of working mainly alone and setting and maintaining your own pace, you may find this kind of work extremely difficult. On the other hand, you may be the kind of student who finds this kind of study attractive.

CONCLUSION

When considering whether or not to enroll in a program based on distance education delivery systems, you obviously need to weigh a number of factors. First, and most important, is whether or not the program will give you what you want and need. Associated closely with this question are the reputation and credibility of the school offering the program. Then there are the normal questions: Is the program staffed by tenure-track faculty or adjuncts or a mix? What kind of library services are available to you? How good are the other support services? What will the program cost? You need to consider these factors just as you would for any other type of program.

Last, there is the question of what education professors like to call "learning styles." How will the teaching format suit you? Some people find asynchronous instruction difficult. It requires a higher degree of self-discipline than synchronous formats. Most people, even experienced students, have never attended school on this basis before. You will have to be comfortable working by yourself in some formats. On the other hand, many adult, professional students find asynchronous formats ideal. They fit their schedules and lifestyles much better than site-based, rigidly scheduled classes. Whether or not distance education will work for you is a question no one else can answer.

REFERENCES

Clark, R. E. (1983). Reconsidering research on learning from media. *Review of Educational Research, 53*(4), 445-459.

Davis, S. (1995). Speaking personally—With Lionel Baldwin. *The American Journal of Distance Education, 9,* 76-81.

Duffy, J. P. (1994). *How to earn an advanced degree without going to graduate school.* New York: Stein & Day.

Russell, T. L. (1995). *The "no significant difference" phenomenon as reported in 214 research reports, summaries, and papers.* Unpublished compilation, North Carolina State University at Raleigh.

Russell, T. L. (1996). Point of view: Technology's threat to the traditional institution—real or imagined? *Journal of Continuing Higher Education, 44*(1), 22-24.

Swenson, C. D. (1995). Graduate degree programs and distance education. *New Directions for Adult and Continuing Education, 67,* 51-60.

4

Up to Speed

*You can lead a man up to the university,
but you can't make him think.*

—Finley Peter Dunne

If you are considering a part-time graduate program—particularly a professional master's—or have just begun one, chances are that someone "led" you to this point. Your employer may have demanded it, or, more likely, encouraged you. Perhaps your company offered to pick up the tuition, which was just too good an opportunity to pass up. Or maybe you yourself read the writing on the wall concerning your career. In any event, some sort of external pressure or stimulus is—or has been—a factor in your decision-making process. But as Dunne's Mr. Dooley notes, once you enter the university, nobody can think for you or even compel you to think at all. Success or failure is in your hands.

A good start is essential, especially in a master's program. Because master's programs are so short in comparison with other degree programs, initial success or failure can create momentum. A poor start is tough to overcome; a poor performance in one class can taint your entire graduate experience. On the other hand, success breeds success.

I've noted several times that your life is almost certainly more complicated than that of full-time, residential graduate students. You have other roles to maintain, two of which, your family and your job, take higher priority. To maintain your multiple roles, you need to prepare carefully for graduate work and to execute it efficiently once you have begun. You will not have the luxury of breaking in slowly. Thus, a good start is crucial. Unfortunately, this brings some hoary old saws to mind, such as "hit the ground running" and developing "a quick learning curve." But, like most clichés, they contain an element of truth.

DEVELOPING A PLAN OF ATTACK

Let's assume you have made the decision to enter a graduate program. Furthermore, you have decided which program, and you have been accepted. For you, reality has suddenly changed. You know you will have to drastically alter your lifestyle. But if you did not intend to succeed, you would not be at this point. How, then, do you quickly become a successful student, particularly if you have been out of school for a few years or if you were not that successful your first time around? Hard work, although obviously necessary, will not be sufficient. You must do some planning, quickly and seriously.

Know the Territory

In formulating a plan of attack, the first logical step is to familiarize yourself with the program requirements. They will vary widely, not only from institution to institution but from program to program. However, most master's programs share some elements. Judith Glazer (1986) listed the following common components:

A core of introductory courses appropriate to the discipline or field of study, such as foundations, theory, or research methods.

A concentration or specialization in a subfield of study, for example, financial accounting, rehabilitation counseling, medical-surgical nursing, or creative writing.

Cognate courses, often outside the department, to broaden the curriculum or to provide needed skills, such as statistics, computer programming, foreign languages, or behavioral sciences.

Integrative experiences to synthesize the program's content and to translate theory into practice, such as seminars, on-campus practicum, internships, and other field work.

Summative experiences to measure the student's achievement and cognitive growth by means of a thesis, research project, comprehensive examination, or a combination of these. (p. 17)

Figure 4.1 is the worksheet for the master's program in higher education (nonthesis) at The University of Iowa. Part A, the foundation courses, represents Glazer's "common core," including a research methods course. This program offers several concentrations, including administrative practices, continuing education practices, and policy studies. Electives (Part E) serve the same purpose as Glazer's cognate courses. The practicum provides an integrative experience. Note that this requirement can be waived for students with professional experience. This stipulation reflects the fact that most of our master's candidates are working, part-time students. Last, the master's project (Part D) and the comprehensive exams (Part F) provide summative components.

You will have the fewest options in scheduling the core, or foundation, courses. To a large extent, they help frame and set a context for the overall program. Your best bet is to take them as soon as possible. Most programs allow somewhat more freedom in developing your area of concentration. And of course, these should be the courses of greatest interest to you. Normally, students are required to take a specified number of courses from an overall category. The prescribed range of courses can be very tight in some fields, such as nursing and electrical engineering, and looser in others, such as education.

The increasing specialization of graduate programs has diminished the number of electives that can be fitted into most master's programs. Therefore, it is important to choose them carefully. On the one hand, they should complement your concentration. On the other, they should broaden your focus. It is for this reason that many departments encourage—or require—that at least one elective course be chosen from another department, perhaps even from a different college. Nursing students in a management concentration, for example, might find elective courses from the business college useful.

COLLEGE OF EDUCATION
HIGHER EDUCATION
M.A.
Minimum Total Semester Hours Required = 32

_____
Student's Name

A. Foundation Courses (9 s.h.)

	Course	Sem/Year	sh Credit
1. 7H:100 (3 s.h.)			

2. One course in research or analytic
    methods such as introductory statistics,
    computer applications, research process,
    and design or survey research:

3. One course in the social context of
    education such as the historical,
    philosophical, political, or sociological
    foundations:

                                                    TOTAL   sh

B. Area of Concentration (14-15 s.h.)
    (Specify concentration)_____

	Course	Sem/Year	sh Credit
1.			
2.			
3.			
4.			
5.			
6.			
7.			
		TOTAL	sh

C. Practicum (2-4 s.h.)
    (May be waived for students with appropriate professional
    experience)

	Course	Sem/Year	sh Credit
1. 7H:333 (2-4 s.h.)			
		TOTAL	sh

D. Project (3 s.h.)
    (Required of all candidates for M.A. degree in higher education.
    Topic to be selected from the area of concentration.)

	Course	Sem/Year	sh Credit
1. 7H:295 (3 s.h.)			
		TOTAL	sh

E. Electives (1-4 s.h.)
    (To be approved by adviser.)

	Course	Sem/Year	sh Credit
1.			
2.			
3.			
		TOTAL	sh

GRAND TOTAL (Must be at least 32 s.h.)   sh

F. Comprehensive Examinations
    (This will consist of six hours of written examinations, based on the core, concentration,
    and specialization according to the plan of study developed individually for each student.
    Students may elect two three-hour exams or three two-hour exams.)

Areas:

1.	Sem/Year
2.	Sem/Year
3.	Sem/Year

_____   _____
Adviser's Signature   Date

Figure 4.1. Master's Program Worksheet, The University of Iowa

As Glazer's description notes, integrative experiences can be quite varied. They range from practicums, which are normally unpaid work experiences in the field under study, to applied seminars and a number of other experiences. Many master's programs, including MBAs, use "capstone" courses as integrative experiences. The Executive MBA program at The University of Iowa, for example, calls this course "Strategic Management and Business Policy." It "explores the nature, scope, and complexity of the chief executive's job, including functional integration of all managerial activities." Purdue University's Krannert School of Management offers an additional integrative component in its executive program. During the final "residency" period, the students take an international trip designed to "provide the participants with a richer comprehension of the global competitive environment through a series of lectures, case analyses, plant visits, outside speakers from government ministries and multinational firms, and associated international business projects." Most integrative experiences, needless to say, are not nearly this exotic or high-powered. But they all have the same purpose, relating theory to practice.

Obviously, the integrative course or experience will come near the end of your program. However, it is a good idea to start planning early. It is not wise to complete your other course work, then ask your adviser, "What can I do now?" Scheduling in a practicum around your work requirements might be difficult. Leaving home to complete it would probably be impossible. And arranging something in a hurry will inevitably mar the experience. Your adviser and you will need to begin exploring options compatible with your location and schedule. Some programs obviate this difficulty by allowing students with considerable experience to waive the practicum requirement, then to take additional course work instead. More creative solutions are sometimes possible. In our Higher Education program at The University of Iowa, we have encouraged some of our students who work in community colleges to set up their practicum in other offices within the same institution. A student working in the continuing education office might arrange a practicum in academic affairs or personnel, for example. If a practicum or internship is a program requirement, early planning can prevent confusion and make the experience considerably more useful and worthwhile.

Although summative experiences are the final component of any graduate degree program, it would be a mistake to wait until the end of your program to begin looking toward them. The most formidable summative experience at the master's level is the thesis. If you are in a program that requires a thesis, do not repeat the mistake of the bulk of graduate students by putting off a decision until you have completed your course work. Begin looking toward it right away.

Make a decision on your topic as early as possible. Use class projects and papers to test possible topics. Once you settle on a topic and clear it with your adviser, everything you do for your classes should lead toward its completion. A bibliographic essay might satisfy a paper requirement in one class; a statement of the problem might make a good project in the next. It is all too easy to look at each course as an obstacle to be checked off as quickly as possible. That attitude actually wastes time in the long run, because one tends to settle on "quick and dirty" projects that will fulfill class requirements with minimum effort. But if you choose that method, your papers and projects and the work you put in on them will be wasted once each course ends.

This piece of advice is not original, of course. When I was a grad student, I heard it and ignored it. I treated each course as an entity and wrote papers that fulfilled requirements. Once graded, they were useless, the hours of work wasted. This conventional stupidity probably cost me 6 months on my master's thesis and a year or more on my dissertation. I hope you will prove yourself smarter than I was.

To a lesser extent, the same admonition holds for other summative experiences, such as master's projects. Although they are not on the same scale as a thesis, planning can save a great deal of time, effort, and even anguish. Even the comprehensive exams that are a part of almost every master's program merit some forethought. Plan to leave every course with a command of the bibliography on which it was based and a good set of notes. Keep all tests and exercises as your professors return them. If you can, reconstruct the questions from your final exams for each course. All of these things will make good review materials for your comprehensive exams.

▓ Executing the Program of Study

Your adviser should have a worksheet similar to that pictured in Figure 4.1. Ask for one. Go over it carefully with your adviser at the beginning of your program. Make sure that both of you keep your copies updated. Learn to think not in terms of one course or semester at a time, but rather of completing the degree. Stephen Covey (1990), the famous time management author, lecturer, and entrepreneur, lists beginning with the end in mind as the second of his "seven habits of highly effective people." This is good advice for any graduate student, particularly the part-timer, who, I maintain, has less margin for error in completing a program of study.

To the greatest extent possible, determine which courses you will take in which semesters or quarters. Start planning for the integrative and summative components. This will be considerably easier if you are in a cohort program, of course. There, you have virtually no options. However, most students can put a program of study together from a variety of courses and formats. This is particularly true in the field of education or if you are in a program located on campus. Either way, plotting and sticking to a schedule offers real advantages, not the least of which is momentum.

As hard as you may try to stay on track, however, the external world may intrude. An illness in the family, a change of jobs, or any number of other things might force you to skip one or more terms. For example, if you are in a cohort but are forced to miss a given course, you may find it difficult to complete your program. Your adviser should be able to help with this. Some options could include independent study or taking the course from another institution—perhaps via distance education—and transferring it in.

▓ Your Load

The pace at which you can proceed may become a major issue. In some programs, you will have no choice. Cohort programs have a built-in assumption that all students will carry the same load of courses. Most executive MBA programs, for example, call on students to take two courses per semester (or the equivalent number of quarter hours). Other programs may promise to deliver only one course per term. However, in such cases, the programs are usually designed so that students can accelerate their progress with other generally available courses or transfer credit.

In the event that you can determine your load, you will almost certainly choose between taking one or two courses per term. It is extremely rare for a student who is working full time to carry more than two courses. The major advantage of taking two courses is obvious; you can finish in half the time. The end will be in sight from the beginning. However, for a fully employed professional, this can represent a strenuous—perhaps excruciating—grind. One course per term is considerably more manageable, in terms of time, energy, and money. But this option means a long overall commitment. So we are back to the controlling cliché, trade-offs.

If your program allows you a choice, consider trying two courses initially. If you find that you can handle the work, you will move fairly quickly. If not, you can, and should, drop back to one course. However, if you initially try just one course, bear in mind that Parkinson's law, "Work expands so as to fill the time available for its completion," will probably apply. You may spend years working below your real capacity. I have known students who have compromised, taking two courses one term and one the next. In this way, they could "reward" themselves for a heavy load one semester with a light one the next. Or they could take two courses most terms but drop back to one for the really difficult courses.

GETTING READY

Advance Work

If you make your decision to go to grad school a month or two in advance of your first class, you will have time to prepare. If you have not written on a regular basis for a few years, it would be a good idea to brush up on your skills. There are any number of books that offer help in this area. Some corporations regularly schedule workshops on the subject. Check with your employer's personnel or training office to see if anything will be available soon. You could do worse than to get a copy of William Strunk and E. B. White's (1979) *The Elements of Style* and review it. I do this every year.

Most programs include a course—usually quantitative in nature—that students universally dread. Education graduate students, for example, fear statistics. Getting a head start by working through a good book on statistics would be time well spent. If nothing else, such an exercise should help reduce your anxiety level.

If you can find the time, read some books on research methodology in your academic field. Although most professional master's programs do not call for major research projects, you will be expected to read, evaluate, and criticize other authors' research in most of your classes.

Familiarizing yourself with the resources of the institution you have chosen will be time well spent. Most university libraries offer tours, even in the evening. Others have made videotapes for the same purpose. Computer labs or centers are also available to students at most universities. If you do not have your own equipment at home, learn the locations and hours of these facilities. If you have the time and interest to take advantage of extracurricular activities or cultural and recreational facilities, check with the appropriate offices. As a student, you may be eligible for substantial discounts on tickets for athletic and cultural events.

If you need someone to point you in the right direction for any of these facilities or services, you can do no better than the secretaries in your home academic department. They know all parts of the campus and have contacts everywhere. Most of them like grad students and are eager to help. However, you can do nothing worse than alienate these people. So mind your manners, and never act like a big shot. They know better.

FACILITIES AND EQUIPMENT

There is no doubt that graduate school involves a major financial commitment, especially if you will have to pay all the bills yourself. Even so, I highly recommend some additional expenses. If you can do so, buy the things that will make your life as a student easier. Given the range of commitments of graduate students who also have full-time jobs, time really *is* money. The things that will save you considerable time will probably be worth every cent you have to pay.

A Home Office

Equip a place to work in your home. This is critical. A traditional student, living on or near campus, can establish a routine centered around university facilities and save money by using its computers, rather than buying one. James Barner (1995) makes a good argument for this strategy in his book, *Conquering Graduate School*. He said, "Living close to campus was a key reason as to why I was able to do so well in graduate school" (p. 112). In large part, this was because he was able to make efficient use of daytime hours, when libraries and computer labs were normally uncrowded. But Barner conceded that spending a great deal of time on campus and depending on campus-based resources was not a good idea for part-time students. He said, and I agree, that working adults, particularly those with families, should work primarily out of their homes.

At many universities, libraries and computer labs are crowded and often noisy at night, not favorable environments for sustained work and concentration. Although you will have to make use of library services, at a minimum, you can plan your visits for maximum effect. By making liberal use of online bibliographic services and copy machines, you can get in, find what you came for, copy or check it out, and leave.

There is no doubt that you will spend less time with your family while in grad school. That is a given. But there is a real difference between being home and studying and being gone. And in most cases, you will already be out of the house for a minimum of one or two nights a week. Unless you absolutely cannot study or write at home due to distractions or lack of space, plan to spend much of your time there.

If at all possible, avoid the hallowed tradition of spreading out your books and papers on the kitchen table after the kids have gone to bed. You can lose considerable start-up time every night. And the prospect of creating havoc in a normally orderly spot breeds procrastination. You want to wait until you are sure you are ready. This is not a good habit for a student who needs to learn to work in short bursts.

It is far better to have a dedicated space in which to work, no matter how cramped or squalid, a variation of Virginia Woolfe's room of one's own. If you live alone or if there are only two of you at home, this should be no problem. If you have kids, however, you will need to work a little harder to set up a work space. Obviously, you start by looking at the least-used room in the house—a guest room, a storage room, or a corner of the basement. I knew one education doctoral student who took over the ping pong table in his basement. His kids, who until then had rarely used it, complained for a week or so but soon got over it. The primary considerations are to locate your study space away from all televisions and radios and, to the extent possible, out of the stream of traffic.

Once you have picked your spot, equip it with the supplies and equipment you expect to use frequently. A comfortable chair is essential. If you try to get by with a leftover kitchen chair or something of that sort, you will find yourself looking for reasons to get up and move around. A good chair is money well spent. The rest of the furniture can, and should, be cheap, unless you have a formal office or study in your home. Your desk, shelves, and filing spaces can be cheap, crude, or even makeshift. Even now, more than 20 years out of grad school, my desk is a defective door, purchased from a lumber yard for $4.00, resting on two discount-store filing cabinets. Both the large work surface and the handy filing space make my work much easier.

The Big Ticket Items

Now comes the expensive suggestion. Get a computer. The time when you are going back to school is probably not the best time to make a major purchase. In fact, it is probably a terrible time. But try to find a way to do it. It need not be the best computer, but at a minimum, you need one that you can use for word processing. Your work must look professional. In other academic programs, you will need additional capabilities—spreadsheets for MBA work, for example. If you depend on university-owned machines, you will have to contend with fierce crowds at the middle and end of each term. Whereas full-time students can usually wait it out, this is not true for students who have full-time jobs. The computer must be there, equipped as you need it, when you are ready to use it.

It is probably not a good idea to count on using your employer's equipment. Although some companies encourage their employees to pursue graduate degrees and to use the company's resources while doing so, this can be a touchy matter. If you doubt that you are welcome to use company equipment or supplies, ask. But remember that "no" definitely means no; even a lukewarm "yes" means no.

Expense is the only reason for not getting your own computer. All other considerations argue for it. Professors used to be pleasantly surprised by professional-looking work; now, they expect it. A computer can save you a great deal of time by making the organization and storage of your work in progress much easier. Backing up your work is easier and more reliable. Rather than photocopying everything, you can back it up on disks and print new copies as needed. But all other factors aside, it will save you innumerable hours of time. And for most working, part-time students, time is even harder to come by than money.

You may also have reasons for acquiring a computer that are not related to school. You are most likely a professional. You are going to find it harder and harder to function in your work without a computer at home. If you have children, they will find it helpful for their school work. And if you throw in a game or two, they will like it even more.

If you should decide to buy a computer or if you already have one, check with your adviser, or any other professors in your department you might know, about whether any specialized software would be useful in the courses you expect to take. If you know students further along in the program, possibly even among your colleagues at work, check with them about what software is vital, as opposed to what is just nice to have.

Having already recommended one major expenditure, I will now suggest another. You will find graduate school much easier to deal with if you have a modem and Internet access, both for e-mail and the World Wide Web. This is especially useful—and more and more frequently necessary—in courses offered at off-campus sites and via distance education. At the very least, it provides another means of communication with the instructor. Increasingly, professors use it to set up class listservs or electronic bulletin boards so that students can communicate with each other as the course proceeds. In the most recent course I taught (via interactive television), we used e-mail to keep discussions going from week to week.

More and more universities are making their library catalogs, serials lists, and other bibliographic services available via the World Wide Web or telnet (direct communication between Internet sites). This provides an excellent means of making your library visits count. By spending some preparatory time online, you can walk into the library and head directly for the items you need, copy or check them out, then head home. And if you are studying at a distance, more and more universities are developing fast turnaround services for books, serial articles, and other materials if students can specify exactly what they need.

Professors are beginning to put more and more materials on the World Wide Web, making them available to students at any time, anywhere. Although this practice is still somewhat limited because of copyright law as well as its relative novelty, it is growing quickly. The catalogs for many collections, particularly government documents, are already available. Although access to the Web obviously is most valuable if you are taking courses off campus or at a distance, it is also useful if your home is in a university town. Often, you can check a data source or a fact as you write in your home, rather than having to put it on a list for your next trip to the library. As I have written this book, I have frequently used the Web to check details on many of the graduate programs I've mentioned. Last, you can often print documents at home, rather than having to stand in line for a copier at the library.

Again, access to e-mail and the Web saves valuable time. Many universities can extend Internet access to their students. Check to see if it is available from the university you have chosen. If not, take a look at the various online services that can provide you with access. They can be expensive, and you will need to keep your use within limits, but the cost should be worth it. If you should not find that to be the case, you could, of course, drop it.

Having urged you to consider securing Internet access, I should also tell you that it can be a double-edged sword. Web surfing and chat rooms are the great time wasters of our age. In my first few days on the Web, I downloaded barbecue and chili recipes, read part of the Unabomber's manifesto, checked baseball scores, and generally enjoyed myself, while hours just disappeared. Needless to say, I was not particularly productive during this time (although one barbecue recipe from North Carolina was great). The point is that if you get Web access, use it to save time. Do not let it become a source of recreation or escapism.

CLASSES

Classes are different in graduate school. Unlike your undergraduate classes, almost everyone will attend almost every time. Like any other graduate students, working adults do not need to be told the importance of going to class. People who pay their way expect to take full advantage of classes. You will be there if at all possible, so I will not insult your intelligence on this point.

Even so, almost everyone with a job and family must miss a class once in a while. Jobs demand travel, kids have to be taken to the emergency room, and toilets back up. In cases of unavoidable absences, manners are important. If you can notify your professor in advance, do so. If an emergency keeps you away, apologize no later than the beginning of the next class. The phone or e-mail, within a day or two, would be better. But I would suggest that you not call a professor at home. Most are reasonably tolerant people used to part-time students and the pressures they work under. It has been my experience, however, that nothing riles professors more than being disturbed at home, especially for something that could be taken care of during office hours.

Also unlike undergraduates, graduate students need to prepare for every class, even the first one. It is a good idea to review the syllabus in advance. If you are taking the course off campus or via a distance education format, you should receive a copy well before the course starts. If you will be attending on campus, ask the professor—or better yet, the departmental secretary—for a copy. Buy at least the main text and read the introduction and the first assignment before you go to the initial session. This is a bit idealistic; not everybody in the class will do so. But if you can, you will find it well worth the effort. At the very worst, you may find out that a given course is not what you thought it was or what you wanted. If so, you will have time to drop it and pick up something else.

▧ Speak Up

Most people are apprehensive about the first session in the first class of a graduate program, especially if they have not attended college in some years. More than likely, you will be somewhat cautious, even intimidated, at first. Get over it as quickly as possible. As a graduate student, you're not there just to listen. You are expected to contribute to the class. It may be unfair, but silence may be taken as an indication of a lack of interest, a lack of preparation, or a lack of competence. Most good professors will try hard to draw out quiet students—but only for so long. Then, they may decide you have lost interest, in which case they will probably lose interest in you. Force yourself to get involved. Among other considerations, graduate school is more enjoyable when you participate. And having some fun can make the rigor and stress considerably easier to deal with.

It is possible to overdo it, of course. You will occasionally find yourself in a class with a student who tries to dominate conversation. Academia breeds a certain amount of showing off. Even the best professors can find it difficult to keep such people from running away with a discussion. The best way to deal with someone like this is to generate participation from as many people in the class as possible. So, if you do your share of the talking and allow others to do theirs, the professor and your colleagues will appreciate it.

When you have questions, try to ask them as they occur to you. In that way, the professor or other students can deal with them in context. If you wait until after class or until the next meeting, the question may no longer seem relevant.

▧ The Killer Class

I mentioned earlier that adults who have been out of school for several years tend to be apprehensive about mathematics-based courses.

And most graduate programs require the completion of one or more such courses. Quantitative methodology courses have long been important in business administration programs and are becoming more so. Students in education and the social sciences must complete statistics-based research methods courses. In advising graduate students, I have found that no other element of the curriculum provokes dread akin to that which accompanies "stat."

You probably will face a course that you and your fellow students consider a killer. Although there are no shortcuts, there are some things you can do. First, do not put it off. If you do, your dread of taking it will only grow. If you have not used math or statistics on a regular basis over the past few years and think you will have to put in more time and practice work on this course, it might be a good idea to reduce your course load during the semester or quarter you take it, if that is an option.

It is also helpful to try not to think of such courses as killers. They are a part of the program for solid academic reasons. They were not included to serve as obstacles to students. The professors who teach stat courses are not sadists. They do not regard them as a means of sorting out students. Indeed, it has been my experience that most of the people who teach quantitative methods courses are well aware of the apprehension of many students and try hard to help them overcome it.

One of the professors in my department who teaches a statistical research methods course begins every session by trying to put his students at ease. He knows they are there because they have to be, and he knows that fear, not a lack of ability, is their major problem. He tries to keep the general stress level down. He advises students that for this course, it is important to prepare for each lecture by carefully doing all assigned readings. He urges them to tape his lectures and to listen to them as often as they need to. He has also found that although most textbooks are similar, students vary in their responses to them. Therefore, he often recommends that students try one of the alternative texts to see if a different way of presenting essentially the same material might be helpful.

Probably most important of all, he urges students to call him. He is used to working professionals and knows that most cannot visit during his office hours. He has become adept at working through problems and concepts on the telephone. In short, the students in our master's programs who take a required course from him do not encounter a fearsome tyrant, intent on making grad students miserable. They find a professor who is anxious that they have a successful and productive learning experience. Although not all professors go as far as he, it is my impression that more often than not, the people who teach the onerous required courses make every effort to help students succeed.

■ Instructional Styles

Classroom styles and routines vary tremendously. Professors develop idiosyncratic methods and manners, of course. But class size, collegiate methodology, and academic disciplines also affect the conduct of classes. And if you choose a program offered through distance education, the basic methodology will vary even more.

Engineering classes are normally large, with instruction based on lectures and labs. If this is your field, I recommend James Barner's (1995) *Conquering Graduate School.* Barner offers much good advice on the dynamics of both large classes and labs. Some MBA programs base their classes on the case-study method. In other disciplines, such as social work and education, most professors use group process models of instruction, normally in classes with small numbers of students. Although you will prefer some styles of class more than others—just as you will like some professors more than others—be prepared to adapt to the varying styles. All have their advantages as well as disadvantages.

■ A Messy Notebook

A discussion of note-taking might seem out of place in a book intended for working professionals. I would like to make a few suggestions anyhow. This is a part of grad school that many students tend to overdo, at least initially. There is an old joke about note-taking among professors: When you say "good morning" to a roomful of freshmen, they say, "good morning"; when you say "good morning" to graduate students, they write it down.

The most effective single thing you can do to make your note-taking effective is to carefully read all assignments in advance. Then, during class, you will have a better grasp of what is and what is not important. You will understand the context of the lecture or discussion and will gain a sense of what you should take down and what you can easily skip. If an assigned reading states a particular argument or interpretation, you will have a better understanding of what is going on when the professor or another student presents a differing point of view. In most classes, you will probably take fewer—but better—notes and give more attention to thinking about the subject at hand than to mechanically trying to write everything down.

Books on succeeding in college often recommend that you recopy or rewrite your notes after each class. And indeed, this is probably a good practice. But most working adults would answer, "Get real!" This is just not going to happen. Getting to the class and taking the notes is tough enough for people on their schedules. When they go home, they still have to tie up the loose ends of the day, then try to get some sleep before work the next day. And when they do have time to work on their classes, they will do so by reading and working on papers, not by redoing work they have done already.

As an alternative to rewriting notes, consider writing them in such a way that invites review and additional commentary. As you take notes, do not try to save paper; leave a lot of blank space. Consider a notebook that is "legal ruled," with about a third of the page to the left of the vertical line. During lectures, take notes only on the right side. Or write only on the front of each notebook page, so that when your notebook is open, your notes are on the right page with the left blank. Then, as soon as you can, review your notes quickly. In the blank space, add any additional comments that either did not occur to you at the time or now seem important. You might even use a different color of ink. Then, each time you review your notes, do the same thing. You will add perspective as time goes by. But the key to doing this is to move quickly. If you start working at it too carefully, you might as well take the time to rewrite all the notes, which would be a real drain on your time. Use of this method of adding to your notes will not give you a neat notebook, of course. Think of it as a work in progress.

If you miss a class and borrow someone else's notes, use them cautiously. In most cases, you will find them of little value. You would probably receive more benefit from discussing the class, however briefly, with the professor or another student. But if you do borrow someone's notes, handle them carefully and return them as quickly as possible. Losing another person's notebook is a capital crime at most universities. If the class is in a distance education format, it was probably videotaped. Try to check out the tape and take notes just as you would if you had been present.

▓ Like Death and Taxes: Final Exams

Exams should be more than a major irritant. From a student's point of view, they should be the last step in a process of planning, reading, attendance, and review. Review means study, of course. There is no substitute for preparation. Like voting in eastern Georgia, where I grew up, study is something best done early and often. I wish it were possible to reveal a new, modern way of preparing for a test, but that would be a fantasy. All of the professors, parents, spouses, and assorted busybodies who have always warned you against last-minute cramming before exams were right. I've spent a lifetime unsuccessfully looking for a loophole.

Some professors, at some universities, contribute to test banks so that current students can get a feel for what their exams are like. If test banks are available, use them. But do not rely on them as a reliable source of questions. If professors intended to give the same questions again, they would not release their exams. Besides, as one of my colleagues says, although he never changes the questions, he does change the answers. What he means is that arguments and interpretations change. In his class, there is not only one answer. He is looking for a well-constructed argument, based on the way his class has proceeded in the current term.

Many students find study groups helpful. Normally, that is more difficult for part-time students, who may have enough trouble merely scheduling classes. However, if some of your colleagues want to get together and if you can all arrange it, you might want to try a study group. It can be a good forum for kicking around ideas and for spotting weaknesses in your own arguments. But group study should never be used as a substitute for individual work; it should only supplement it.

▓ Grades

Grading is different in graduate school. A "C" is a failing grade. You probably could not survive more than one in the course of a master's program. You will need to maintain at least a "B+" average, but do not settle for that. Start each course determined to earn an "A." A couple of "B's" or "B+'s" will not kill you, but you will want to keep them to a minimum.

Avoid the "I" (Incomplete) like the plague. At times, taking one will seem seductive. You will hear some of your classmates, or even yourself, say, "If I could just take another month, this would be a great paper," or "The crash project at work fouled me up; I can finish the paper for this course in the opening weeks of the next term, before those courses get intense." These are common, rational responses to the pressures that can make completing a course difficult. But it is unwise to give in to them. Deferring the stress now will compound it later. This can really foul you up, especially if you are in a cohort program.

SOME GOOD NEWS

My academic home is in adult education, a discipline concerned in part with analyzing the differences between adult and juvenile students and developing the most effective instructional strategies for the former group. Much of the research in this field concerns the relative efficacy of various teaching and learning formats and styles, both in terms of objective results ("outcomes") and student satisfaction.

Many of the things we have learned seem obvious. Adult students generally want to be treated as adults, a preference that grows stronger over time. Adults tend to be more goal oriented than younger students, and they look for immediate opportunities to apply course content. Also, they bring valuable experience to the classroom; professors and other students learn from them. All of this is grossly oversimplified, of course, but it is generally helpful in designing educational programs for adults.

It has been my experience that the differences between the learning styles and preferences of adults and college students of a traditional age have caused a great deal of anxiety, discomfort, and even insult, but mainly at the undergraduate level. And even there, this is rapidly changing. For the most part, the teaching strategies that professors have customarily used for graduate students are not only compatible with what we know about adult learning styles and preferences, they are complementary. Many professors particularly enjoy working with part-time, adult students, whose experience in the professional world can, and does, enrich the educational process. It is not uncommon for professors eventually to prefer working with this group. And graduate students, whether full-time or part-time, generally recognize the relevance of the curriculum to their career goals. If not, they leave.

In the end, however, the quality of the experience comes back to the same critical factor, the institution. Faculty in programs for part-time graduate students offer the range of characteristics—good and bad—of the faculty overall. In the three state universities for which I have worked, the faculty members have run the gamut from brilliant to incompetent, from truly inspirational to boring. Our programs for working adult students have reflected these characteristics. In each case, the brilliant and inspirational have far outnumbered the incompetent and boring.

More than any other factor, your choice of institution will govern the quality of instruction you receive. As at any other level of formal education, you will prefer some professors to others. There will probably be one class you dislike intensely. But that, of course, is no different for part-time students than for anyone else. Most of the time, you will want to simply ride out a course with a poor professor and hope for a better one next time. However, you are the customer. If a course is intolerable, drop it. If the quality of instruction in your program is poor, find another one.

Overall, if you are in a good school, you should find your interaction with the faculty members pleasant and rewarding. You will be exposed to some excellent minds, and they will, in most cases, respect the experience and expertise you are bringing to their classrooms.

REFERENCES

Barner, James. (1995). *Conquering graduate school: What you need to know.* Plainfield, IL: Wishbone.

Covey, S. (1989). *Seven habits of highly effective people: Restoring the character ethic.* New York: Simon & Schuster.

Glazer, J. (1986). *The master's degree: Tradition, diversity, innovation.* Washington, DC: Association for the Study of Higher Education.

Strunk, W., & White, E. B. (1979). *The elements of style.* New York: Macmillan.

5

REGULATIONS AND RESOURCEFULNESS

Just say "no."
—Nancy Reagan

In Chapter 1, I commented on the philosophical dimension of the tension between the traditional, or arts and sciences, graduate school model and the newer model of professional development and credentialing. In particular, I noted Judith Glazer's 1986 pronouncement that the professional master's degree had become the "new paradigm" in graduate study. Not only had this model emerged, she said, it now dominated master's-level study. Furthermore, part-time study had become the predominant mode of pursuing this type of degree. She was not the first critic to comment on this change. As early as 1983, Jaroslav Pelikan pointed to the ways in which the predominance of the professional master's and part-time students had changed the nature of graduate study. The days in which graduate schools could successfully represent themselves as academia's "Bureau of Standards" (p. 13) had ended, he warned. Critics such as Pelikan and Glazer correctly noted the more practical focus of curricula and the utility of substituting practica and projects for master's theses given the makeup and goals of the largest part of the graduate student population. However, in many ways, the prevailing mindset of the university remains the same. Many universities, particularly the large state and private research institutions, continue to treat the part-time student as a marginal presence, an aberration at worst, a slight nuisance at best.

Allan Knox (1993), one of the leading scholars in the field of adult education, considers the traditional research university model so firmly entrenched that efforts at reform are hopeless: "Part-time study in credit courses is constrained by requirements, procedures, and expectations that have evolved in preparatory education programs for young, full-time students and that are imposed on adult education programs to assure 'quality' " (p. 31). In his view, traditional institutions are incapable of innovation of the sort that can effectively serve part-time, adult populations.

Although Knox may be overly critical, it is nevertheless true that many institutions are not particularly user-friendly to part-time students, despite their numbers and their impact on the curriculum. Indeed, when issues relating to change are raised within a university, it is usually the office of the graduate dean that adopts Nancy Reagan's simple and nostalgic slogan, "Just say 'no.' "

This adherence to tradition has provoked opposition in some parts of major universities. It is one of the reasons (but by no means the only one) many colleges of business have pursued professional school status in order to run their graduate programs independently of the graduate dean.

Although engineering colleges have not taken this tack, they have successfully pioneered in the development of professional degrees, taken the lead in serving off-campus audiences, and led the way in adopting distance education formats. Often, they have done so counter to the direction preferred by graduate colleges. I believe they have done this—and succeeded—for several reasons. More than most professors, the engineering faculty members have shown a genuine commitment to the professional development of practicing engineers. They have enjoyed the financial support of many large employers who have been willing to subsidize such efforts. And the rigor of engineering colleges at most major universities is unchallenged; they enjoy great credibility. Thus, specious or fallacious arguments about quality and standards had little effect. Other colleges within U.S. universities have generally not been so fortunate.

In this chapter, I will discuss some of the nuts-and-bolts consequences of the reflexive defense of tradition, in the name of "standards" in graduate education. They include such things as residency requirements, proscriptions or limitations of some modes of instruction, and overall time limits, all of which have a disproportionately adverse effect on part-time students. In adult education textbooks, these consequences are called "barriers." Most, however, are merely nuisances. It is important to realize that a fair number of these consequences are easily overcome. Some are worth complaining about, others can only be tolerated.

THE BARRIERS:
READ THE CATALOG

As you begin your program, get the graduate catalog and read it. Do not just skim it; familiarize yourself with it. This is a necessary step in your effort to avoid hassles in grad school, but it is not sufficient. At most universities, this catalog is not the definitive word: It is more like a baseline. Colleges and departments may add additional rules, requirements, and stipulations. These additional conditions may apply to virtually anything, from admissions to dismissal.

At most places, the rules in effect at the time you enter are those under which you will graduate, if you proceed at a specified pace. That is, rule changes normally are not retroactive. This is important to keep in mind as you proceed. If a rule should change after your admission, especially if its effect is unfavorable, you should be prepared to point out the terms under which you entered your program. You have a greater interest in keeping track of such regulations than the professors, program coordinators, and secretaries with whom you will deal.

Try to get an accurate and complete picture before beginning your program. Read all collegiate and departmental rules and policies that may augment the graduate catalog. If you have questions, ask your academic adviser or, in some cases, the program coordinator or professional adviser.

▓ Residency Requirements:
The Mother of All Barriers

Perhaps more than any other vestige of the traditional arts and sciences graduate study model and more than any other facet of the inertia of university bureaucracies, residency requirements tend to bedevil part-time graduate students, complicating their lives and slowing their progress toward graduation. Therefore, I will deal with the residency question at length.

Residency requirements can be as complex and vexing as any issue a part-time graduate student will ever face. Many universities continue to maintain them, even for professional master's degree programs, where they can be counterproductive. It is critical that you understand exactly how the residency requirements of your institution work. The term means different things at different places.

Sometimes, "residency requirement" means that a certain number of credit hours must be taken on campus. Other times, the same term means that courses must be taught by a member of the graduate faculty, or that it cannot be a correspondence course, or that a certain number of classes must be taken after formal admission. Occasionally, it means that a student must take a full-time load for one or more semesters. To confuse matters further, the term sometimes means two or more of these at the same time. At The University of Iowa, for example, we have three residency rules. First, most—but not all—master's programs require a minimum of 8 hours of registration in courses offered on campus. The second residency rule requires that 24 hours of a 32-hour program be taken after admission and that none of those hours can be earned by transfer or correspondence study. The third specifies that doctoral candidates must take a minimum of two semesters, 9 hours each, in residence at the Iowa City campus.

▓ Life in the Magic Kingdom

Residency requirements exist for the purpose of forcing students to experience the culture of the institution. As such, they represent the values of the traditional PhD program model. According to the rationale for residency requirements, students need to make the campus the core of their existence, at least for a while. If they do not drink beer with professors and other students, do not attend symposiums in the evenings, and do not become members of the student class, the argument goes, they miss invaluable experiences and socialization as graduate students. As an official of the American Association of University Professors put it, "They can't immerse themselves fully into the academic program" (Taylor, 1993, p. 23). Those of us who work in continuing education and promote part-time, off-campus, and distance education programs refer to this as the "magic kingdom syndrome," a sincere belief among academics that if someone can walk among us and breathe the air we breathe, his or her life and intellect will be improved.

This argument is not entirely without merit. Campus life is enjoyable, usually stimulating, and sometimes exciting. It is probably true that most people would prefer a temporary immersion in the campus culture, if at all possible. That people who cannot become full-time resident students will miss something truly valuable is an arguable point. But saying a graduate education is somehow flawed without living in the magic kingdom is untrue. It is not necessary, and its absence in no way degrades either the degree you will earn or the education it represents.

No one has ever proven that some recipients of a given master's degree are lesser nurses, engineers, managers, naval officers, or school superintendents because they missed some of the ancillary pleasures of the university culture. I do not believe anyone could prove this. Indeed, there are some indications that directly contradict this view.

The Council on Social Work Education, the specialized agency that accredits graduate social work programs, until recently demanded a one-year residency requirement of its member schools. However, the Council examined several studies on the effect of the requirement and "failed to find evidence that part-time programs were inferior to full-time programs" (Butler, 1993, p. 211). Indeed, one of the investigators concluded, "Most current empirical evidence suggests that part-time students equal or exceed full-time students in academic achievement or field work performance" (Potts, 1992, p. 72). As a result of these studies, the Council no longer requires any full-time on-campus enrollment. Unfortunately, social work schools at some universities have been unable to offer this option to their students due to local graduate college rules.

▓ The Law Is the Law

Tradition dies hard. Although many universities have provisions for waivers of such requirements, it is sometimes difficult to obtain them at both the departmental and collegiate levels. Even as universities are beginning to offer more and more off-campus and distance education programs for the benefit of part-time students, academic departments or graduate colleges are imposing residency requirements as a sort of trade-off for agreeing to the innovation. I have been involved in the development of several programs in which departmental faculty held off-campus delivery hostage to a residency requirement. Rather than killing the entire program, I have generally given in on this issue. Needless to say, however, such strictures have had a negative effect on the popularity—and thus the utility—of such programs.

To the graduate dean and part of the faculty, residency requirements recall a nostalgic ideal, the way graduate school was when they went through. For working adults, however, particularly those in professional master's programs, they represent serious barriers. They serve no useful purpose and certainly none bolstered by any kind of empirical evidence. Many universities still enforce them, but they have nonetheless lost the ability to make them effective.

For example, let's consider two students working toward master's degrees in education. Both live in the same town, about 75 miles from the university where they will earn their degrees. The first is in a counselor education program, offered at several sites via interactive television. She attends classes at a site 10 minutes from her home and takes one course per term. The classes are offered on a synchronous basis; she interacts with her professor and the other students in real time. In fact, some of her fellow students are on the main campus, with her professor. Even so, she will face a requirement that she take 8 semester hours while sitting in a classroom on the main campus.

The other student in her town is in an educational administration program. He, too, takes one course per term. Because his program is not available via television, he drives to campus one night per week, which takes him a little less than 2 hours. His boss lets him leave work half an hour early so that he can make it to class on time. After the class, dog-tired, he drives home. He does not spend one minute more than necessary on campus; he has to be at work early the next morning. Therefore, he has no more exposure to the academic culture than does his colleague in counselor education. However, unlike her, because he attends classes on campus, he will not be inconvenienced by the residency requirement.

It would be absurd to claim that the residency requirement would have any real impact on either student in such a situation. The latter student gains no more from so-called residency than the former. Each student is simply doing what it takes to earn the degree, taking advantage of the best arrangement available. In fact, to clear the residency requirement, the former student will probably drive to campus for two semesters, just like the latter, even though she could take the same courses in her home town. It is unlikely that she will spend more time on campus than he does.

In fact, the situation could become even more absurd. She might take precisely the same course on campus as she could have taken at home. She will be in the same classroom as the professor, but otherwise, she will have the same experience as she would have had in her home town. The only difference will be a 2-hour drive each way. Actually, it is likely that her professor, being a decent and sensible sort, will see the absurdity of the situation and tell her to attend the classes at the remote site near her home while he carries her on the roll of the on-campus section.

This scenario might seem absurd, but it is real. It is taking place now. In this case and many variations, the residency requirement does not contribute to the quality of education; it serves only to irritate or confound. Such requirements may conceivably serve a useful purpose at the undergraduate or doctoral levels—though I doubt it—but they are only barriers in professional master's programs.

▓ Living With the Law

If you face a residency requirement in the pursuit of your degree and believe that it is a nuisance, serving no useful purpose in your education, you are probably correct. Nonetheless, it is a fact of life; your chances of escaping it are slim. You need to begin making plans to satisfy it. If you are in an evening program, on a campus, the odds are that you will not have to contend with a residency requirement. However, it is possible that there may be one or two courses—either required or that you want badly—that are simply not scheduled for evening delivery. You may need to figure out how to get onto campus during the day for a semester or two, even if you have to work out some sort of agreement with your employer. The same is probably true if you are in a weekend program; residency, per se, should not be an issue.

If, however, you are taking your program at an off-campus site or center or via a distance education format, you may well be required to register for a specified number of hours on campus. This is frequently the case in education programs in particular. There are several options for dealing with this problem.

First, many programs offer summer session courses, often on an accelerated schedule. You may be able to earn as many as 3 semester hours in an intensive 3-week course, or 6 or 8 hours in a longer session. Summer sessions of this sort were originally designed for teachers, who could come to campus full time when school was out of session. This strategy will not work for everyone, however. Fewer and fewer people, even in the field of education, can get away for extended periods in the summer. However, given your alternatives, this might be the best way to clear the residency requirement, even if it should require a leave of absence from your job.

Another possibility is to register on campus for practicum, master's project, or thesis hours, then return home and do the work there. Many students use this route to clear at least a large part of their residency requirement. This defeats the whole purpose of a residency requirement, of course. But as we have seen, the requirement itself is just another part of academia in which form and sentimentality sometimes outweigh substance and utility. Defeating the purpose of a useless rule does no harm.

LESSER BARRIERS

State Residency

If you decide to attend a state-supported university, your legal residence may become an issue. Obviously, you will want to avoid out-of-state tuition, if at all possible. There are several possibilities. First and most likely, you probably qualify already. Although laws and regulations vary from state to state, most specify that you must have lived in that state for a given period, usually 6 to 12 months, but not in a student status. Second, at many public universities, you can take a limited load, perhaps up to 4 or 5 credit hours, without being assessed out-of-state tuition. For many students in professional master's programs, this will be sufficient.

If you live near the border of two states, it is possible that the public universities offer reciprocity on in-state tuition. Or sometimes, the member institutions of bistate or multistate consortiums have negotiated mutual waivers of out-of-state tuition.

Once you have qualified for in-state tuition, by whatever means, your status should not change over the course of a degree program.

▓ Transfer Credits

Even though the issue of transfer credits will be evaluated and ruled on at the time of your admission, this issue can still be touchy. For example, the graduate college might have credited you with a given number of transfer hours. However, if they do not fit within a program of study as established by your adviser and approved by departmental faculty, those credits will be useless. Therefore, you should plan to sketch out a program of study with your adviser as soon as possible. Be sure he or she gives you a definitive answer about the applicability of transfer credits.

Your adviser should have some flexibility on this issue. If you can point out just how the transfer course or courses could complement your current program, he or she might find your argument persuasive. Although such course work might not relate directly to your concentration, you might be able to make a case for its acceptance as an elective. You have paid for earlier coursework; make every possible effort to use it. But whether these credits are allowed or not, you need to know going in exactly how many courses, and credit hours, remain.

▓ Time Limits

Universities and their graduate colleges are big on time limits. You will find many references to them in your graduate catalog and supplementary collegiate and departmental materials. Become familiar with all of them. Some can have a disproportionate effect on part-time students.

Your school will probably have some sort of overall limit on the total number of years allowed to earn a degree. For example, a university may specify that all credits must have been earned within a defined period, perhaps no longer than 8 to 10 years before the term you intend to graduate. Sometimes, these limits are mandated by accrediting associations. For example, the Council on Social Work Education requires its member schools to enforce a four-year limit for the MSW (Butler, 1993). Overall time limits such as these apply to full-time and part-time students alike. Although you certainly do not want to take anything like 10 years to earn your degree, a rule like this might invalidate some credits you had earned in an earlier attempt at grad school. This is particularly important to keep in mind if you transferred in some hours from another school. Just because they were accepted at the time of your admission does not mean that they will be applicable indefinitely.

If you should choose not to enroll for an extended period, typically 12 months, you may be required to apply for readmission. When that happens, the university will probably recheck your eligibility for in-state tuition, sometimes asking pointed questions about the period during which you were not enrolled. Letters demanding that respondents "Give us a chronological account (including summers) of your major activities since you were last enrolled" make sense to full-time resident students who left town and are now returning. However, to adult students who are living in the same house as before, working at the same job, but who may have had to drop out for a year because of job or family problems, such questions—with no apparent connection to anything—can seem inane at best, annoying or insulting at worst. If you should ever receive such an aggressive query, do not take it personally; the form was not designed with people like you in mind. Accept it for what it is and answer it promptly and fully.

Some schools have continuous enrollment rules that apply after all course work is completed. That means that after a student has completed all classroom work, he or she must register each term (usually excluding summers) until he or she completes all requirements. In short, it means that if a student takes more than one semester or quarter to complete a thesis, a master's project, or comprehensive exams, he or she must pay tuition each of those terms (such rules ordinarily do not require registration in summer terms). This will usually not be an issue in a nonthesis program. However, it is possible that you might not complete a master's project or practicum in a single semester. Check on the rules before you complete your thesis or project. The monetary penalty may prove to be a powerful incentive. If you must extend such work over more than one term, register for absolutely the fewest hours allowed.

Should you ever have to take a grade of "Incomplete," which I strongly advise against, be extremely careful about time limits. At some schools, you are allowed a specified period in which you can clear the incomplete by replacing it with a grade. A year is not uncommon. Other schools do not have strict time limits but will convert any standing incomplete to an "F" when a student registers for another class or term. This is something you cannot allow to happen. Besides the waste of time, money, and effort, the damage to your grade-point average would be devastating.

Probation and Dismissal

When a graduate student begins to get into academic trouble, the first official action is a letter stating that he or she is "not meeting standards." These standards are fairly subjective and are normally defined at the departmental level. But any grade below "B," or even too many "B's," could prompt such a notice. And because part-time students take so few hours, their academic shortcomings are more obvious.

Normally, a student who receives an academic warning is given a specified period of time in which to demonstrate improvement. If that improvement is not forthcoming, he or she will be dismissed. Obviously, you must do everything possible to avoid this situation in the first place.

If you should ever receive such a warning, take it seriously. Carefully reconsider your goals, your ability, and your level of commitment. If it is possible that you lack either the ability or the willingness required to succeed, it will be time to give it up, at least temporarily. The sacrifices required by graduate study are too great to endure in a losing cause.

Discriminatory Fees

Most colleges and universities raise their tuition levels on an annual basis. However, they face varying degrees of pressure to keep the increases as low as possible. Boards of regents or trustees concerned about public relations or political reaction serve as real checks on tuition levels. To raise needed cash, colleges and universities frequently impose fees for ancillary goods and services. And these fees generally hit part-time students disproportionately, sometimes ridiculously so.

Student activities fees are a nearly universal fixture in higher education. They are used to support campus organizations, recreational facilities, and such activities as the newspaper and yearbook. They can hit part-time students doubly hard. First, part-time students generally make limited use of the services and activities these fees support. In many cases, because hours and location are always geared to the traditional student, they are not even accessible. And even if they are available, such things as foreign film series and pep rallies rarely interest adults. Second, at many universities, the fee remains at the same dollar level, regardless of the number of hours in which a student is registered. Therefore, over the duration of a master's degree, part-time students will pay proportionately much more in activities fees than their full-time counterparts.

More and more schools are instituting computer fees to help keep up with the enormous costs of academic computing. Again, the part-time student normally will use computing facilities less but pay more. University computer labs are simply not practicable for many, if not most, working students.

Sometimes, computer-use fees are assessed at a flat rate, regardless of the number of hours for which a student is registered; sometimes, they operate on a sliding scale. But even then, the part-time student pays more. In one midwestern university, for example, a full-time graduate student will be assessed a $46.00 fee, per semester, for taking a 12-hour load. A part-time student taking one course will pay $23.00. Thus, the former pays $3.83 a credit hour in computer fees, and the latter pays $7.67. Over a 32-hour master's program, the full-time student will pay $127.00, the part-timer $253.00.

Some universities charge a fee to help defray the cost of operating health services. Like other fees, this one—even if it is prorated—tends to cost part-time students disproportionately more money. Often, however, it is a flat fee, regardless of a student's status. And if few part-time students use computer labs, even fewer ever use health services.

First, student health services are often closed in the evening. Second, the working professionals who make up the greatest share of part-time grad students already have coverage through their employers; it is part of their compensation. When they need medical service, they go to providers specified or approved by their group insurance plans. Thus, from the perspective of a university's health service, working adults are the perfect customers. They pay fees but demand no service. Any insurance company would drool at the prospect of signing up such a group.

As irritating as miscellaneous user fees can be, they are usually relatively cheap. In most cases, it is probably best just to pay them. Realistically, you have few alternatives. However, when you are considering programs, always be sure to ask about fees as well as tuition. Get the real cost before making a final commitment. You can also try to take advantage of the services offered, whenever possible.

Your student activities fees may entitle you to discounted tickets to athletic and cultural events, for example.

Sometimes, complaining helps. I am aware of one university that instituted a flat-rate health fee for all students but had to partially back down when hundreds of part-time students raised a furor. That will not always happen, of course, but sometimes complaints have a cumulative effect. Your protest may be one of many that will eventually help a subsequent generation of part-time students.

Some people have expressed their displeasure in another way. I know of several graduates who, on receiving fund-raising letters from their school's alumni associations, have written back, detailing the fees they paid for services they did not receive and explaining that donations to the university would not be forthcoming for a few years, if ever.

DON'T TAKE IT PERSONALLY

The degree to which you will have to deal with bureaucratic rigidity, inconsistency, and ambiguity in your graduate program will depend to a great extent on the type of institution you have chosen. Smaller, specialized schools tend to be more focused and coherent and, therefore, comprehensible and efficient. Large universities incline toward decentralized administration. And decentralization inevitably breeds confusion. As noted in Chapter 2, administrative simplicity is not always desirable. The vitality and reputation of a large university can more than justify the accompanying administrative complexity.

Many years ago, I attended Naval Officer Candidate School, an institution noted for its adherence to rules and regulations. Many seemed overly rigid, odd, pointless, or counterproductive. One of the most important things my fellow students and I learned was to react to the petty rules and rituals by laughing them off as "just part of the harassment." This was an old saying, passed from one generation of officer candidates to the next. Simply put, it meant that none of the regulations were personal, many of them need not be taken too seriously, and coming to grips with bureaucracy was one element of learning to live and function within a complex organization.

If and when you face conflicting rules, outdated policies, and even stubbornness and stupidity, do not take it personally. You are not being singled out. Often, when part-time graduate students run afoul of a university bureaucracy, they become frustrated. If you think straightening out details seems more complicated than it should be, you may be right. But it is not because people want to cause you trouble. It is usually because your distance from campus or your part-time status or both mean that routine procedures aren't applicable, and this can disconcert some university personnel.

Full-time students also have their share of problems, but for two reasons, their difficulties frequently do not seem as severe. First, full-time students tend to be younger and more acculturated to the institutional environment. Things that may strike an outsider as strange can seem normal to people on the inside. Second, when something goes wrong, full-time students can immediately go to the appropriate office or offices and begin to deal with it. Unlike part-timers, they enjoy a day-to-day knowledge of the institution and an easy access to its bureaucracy. Students who work during the day and can come to campus only in the evening—when all the offices are closed—or who live far from the campus and cannot visit at all, generally find it more difficult to reach the appropriate office. Their phone calls may be bounced from office to office. This can make resolving the situation slower and more complex, which can make the offending rule or policy *seem* personal.

Although some policies certainly have a disproportionately negative effect on part-time students, they are almost never the result of malice but rather, of the lingering dominance of the traditional, arts and sciences-oriented PhD model of graduate school. In many large universities, part-time grad students remain an afterthought, a condition reflected in the operative rules and policies.

When dealing with a large university, it is important to understand that there is no one person or office in charge. To complete a graduate program and to cope with problems that come up along the way, a grad student may have to deal with half a dozen, or even more, administrative offices. Mark Rossman (1995) wrote a book for prospective graduate students with the title *Negotiating Graduate School.* His title captures the reality of the process of earning a graduate degree.

As you negotiate graduate school, resourcefulness and a sense of humor will be your most valuable assets. Learn the rules. This will frequently give you an advantage. Try to laugh off inconsequential issues. When you believe you should make an issue of a rule or policy, keep at it until you reach the person who actually has the ability and authority to deal with your problem. If you lose at that level, it would probably be wise to accept the fact and move on. Sustained battles have a tendency to distract students; they are rarely worth the effort.

DEALING WITH THE GOOD GUYS

You will never be left entirely on your own. There are a number of people charged with helping you. The most important, of course, will be your academic adviser. He or she will be a professor whose job is to help you choose your courses, stay on task, and put together committees, when necessary. His or her job applies to all things academic. However, helping you deal with ornery bureaucrats in other parts of the university is not their role, and ordinarily, you should not expect them to get involved in "administrivia."

To help grad students negotiate administrative tangles, many programs also employ professional advisers. These are student service professionals whose job is to deal with all of the administrative details of your program. Large departments may have advisers who deal specifically with their off-campus or evening programs. If not, the same person who handles the daytime, residential program should also serve part-time students.

If your program is offered in conjunction with a continuing education division, as many evening, off-campus, and distance education degrees are, you will have another person to go to for information and assistance, the program coordinator (the title may vary somewhat). Although these people generally have little authority or decision-making power, they know and are in touch with the people who do. They are often the quickest and best source of information and assistance.

Experienced program coordinators become expert in diagnosing administrative problems. With their networks of contacts in virtually every office on campus, they can usually move toward resolving problems in short order. In a given day, a continuing education program coordinator may resolve a dispute over a grade of "incomplete" with the registrar, talk with the graduate dean's office about a program of study discrepancy, call the bookstore to find out why books have not been shipped to an off-campus site, discuss camera angle problems with video technicians, and attend to dozens of other details.

Serving as an intermediary and advocate for students is an important part of the job description for both professional advisers and program coordinators. Although they normally have little influence on the policies that govern graduate study, they are often highly effective at problem solving. Many become unabashed champions of working, adult students.

There is one more group of university employees who can do you a lot of good—collegiate and departmental administrative assistants and secretaries, as I have noted earlier. They know the rules and procedures better than most professors. They have friends or colleagues in other offices whom they can call on for quick assistance. And, for the most part, they tend to like, or at least tolerate, graduate students. Treat these people as the professionals they are. Never insult or patronize them. For if they have the ability to help you—which they do—they also have the ability and the knowledge of university mechanics to make your life much less pleasant.

When a problem with a support or service office occurs, you can choose to deal with it in a couple ways. Obviously, you can try to call the office in question directly. This may work, but it may not. To a clerk in the registrar's office, for example, part-time students are usually a very small part of the overall population. He or she, therefore, may not be familiar with the nuances and accommodations that are part of some programs. You stand a good chance of being bounced around from one office to another. Although this could be regarded as a sign of equitable treatment—resident full-time students frequently are treated in just this way—such a rationalization might be of little comfort. If you are calling from home, you may get pretty frustrated as you imagine your phone bill piling up. If you are trying to deal with a problem from work, your boss may eventually get tired of seeing you distracted from your job.

A better means of dealing with administrative problems is to find an advocate, namely the professional adviser, program coordinator, or departmental secretary. It is much easier, and usually more effective, to enlist these professionals and paraprofessionals to help you square away details than it is to call office after office yourself. They know the local codes and customs and can usually cut through the confusion quickly. Actually, if you can make the right ally, you will probably face fewer hassles than if you were on campus, being sent from office to office, which is the norm for the full-time student.

ON YOUR SIDE

Universities, like any other complex organizations, depend on set, stated procedures and policies. Without some order, they could not work at all. However, because they are complex and because their administration is to a greater or lesser degree decentralized, the actual administration of these written and unwritten guides depends on human interaction. When a university accepts you, it says it believes that you can succeed in completing your degree. No one there wants to stop you. Even for the part-time student, a lot of people are there to help you.

REFERENCES

Butler, A. C. (1993). The impact of the 1-year residency requirement on students preferring part-time study. *Journal of Social Work Education, 29,* 212-223.

Glazer, J. (1986). *The master's degree: Tradition, diversity, innovation.* Washington, DC: Association for the Study of Higher Education.

Knox, A. B. (1993). *Strengthening adult and continuing education: A global perspective on synergistic leadership.* San Francisco: Jossey-Bass.

Pelikan, J. (1983). *Scholarship and its survival: Questions on the idea of graduate education.* Princeton, NJ: Princeton University Press.

Potts, M. K. (1992). Adjustment of graduate students to the educational process: Effects of part-time enrollment and extracurricular roles. *Journal of Social Work Education, 28,* 61-76.

Rossman, M. (1995). *Negotiating graduate school.* Thousand Oaks, CA: Sage.

Taylor, V. (1993, July 15). Part-time grad students feel the social and academic pinch. *Black Issues in Higher Education,* 22-24.

6

Baby Needs Shoes

Financing Part-Time Study

▨▨▨▨▨▨▨▨▨▨▨▨▨▨▨▨▨▨▨▨▨▨▨▨▨▨

Follow the money.
—"Deep Throat" to Bob Woodward

For many professionals considering an advanced degree, the timing could not be worse. Old loans for undergraduate study, new mortgages, and young families compete for the dollars needed for tuition. And to a great extent, these students are on their own. Federal and university tuition policies, as well as financial aid priorities, are heavily stacked against part-time students, particularly at the master's level. Almost three quarters of all part-time master's candidates receive no support at all, not even loans (U.S. Department of Education [USDE], 1995). Only a small minority receive financial assistance from external sources, as is shown in Table 6.1.

For the majority of part-time, working graduate students, financial considerations were foremost in their decisions to pursue an advanced degree. I do not mean to depreciate the intrinsic value of graduate study, of course. Unless you respect and value the degree you are considering and the academic discipline it represents, it would be

TABLE 6.1   Percentage of Part-Time, Part-Year, or Both Types of Master's Students Who Received Financial Aid, by Source of Aid and Institution Type: 1992 to 1993

College Type	Any Aid	Federal	State	Institutional	Other	Employer
Public	26.1	9.8	2.5	11.7	8.0	6.7
4-year non-doctorate-granting	18.8	6.6	2.4	5.5	7.5	6.5
4-year doctorate-granting	30.4	11.7	2.5	15.3	8.2	6.7
Private, not for profit	31.4	11.0	0.4	10.3	14.9	11.8
4-year non-doctorate-granting	28.3	9.1	0.6	6.9	14.7	11.2
4-year doctorate-granting	33.1	11.9	0.4	12.1	15.0	12.1

Source: U.S. Department of Education, National Center for Education Statistics (1995).

better not to undertake it. However, intrinsic value alone rarely moves a graduate degree to the top of the priority list for fully employed people. Unless the long-range financial gain promises to outweigh the considerable short-term sacrifices, most gainfully employed people find graduate study's intrinsic value alone an insufficient motivation for the considerable sacrifices entailed. This is doubly true for people with families.

In the most extreme cases, such as military officers, extrinsic pressures can be everything. For them, the master's is a check-off item. Where an officer earns his or her degree has no financial implications. But not earning it does. Without it, the captain (Army, Air Force, Marine Corps) or lieutenant (Navy, Coast Guard) will never make major or lieutenant commander. His or her career will end. Needless to say, this would have profound financial consequences.

Beyond the initial decision to attend graduate school on a part-time basis, financial considerations are almost always factors as people decide among programs and determine where, how, and at what rate of progress to complete them. The comparative reputations of MBA programs, for example, vary widely, which tends to have an unpredictable, but significant, impact on career development and eventual financial return. On the other hand, teachers can precisely calculate the financial advantage of earning a master's or specialist's degree, but the source of the degree is rarely a factor.

Costs are sometimes a factor in determining whether to commute to a campus or to take courses via distance education. And the rate of tuition and related expenses can affect your pace toward the degree.

If you have read this far, you have probably already decided that the combination of intrinsic and extrinsic rewards justifies the cost of beginning graduate school. You know that costs will be an important issue for the duration of your program of study and perhaps afterward, if you should decide to borrow money. Therefore, it is appropriate to consider some of the details of the costs and ways of minimizing them. Also, this chapter will deal with the availability— however limited—of financial aid, the advisability of borrowing money, and the ways in which to maximize your employer's interest in your education.

THE MATTER OF COSTS

Graduate education is not cheap. Data from the most recent National Postsecondary Student Aid Study (NPSAS; USDE, 1995) indicate that part-time master's students worked an average of 36.9 hours per week while taking courses. The implication is that most worked full time. Those who attended public institutions paid an average of just over $1,600 per year in tuition and fees, out of an average income of $35,200, or 5% of their incomes. Similar students who chose private universities paid an average annual tuition of $3,400, or 8% of their average incomes of $41,000. A more detailed breakdown of average tuition and income comparisons is shown in Table 6.2.

Although these costs are certainly significant, they are not all-inclusive. They do not include books, for example, which can easily run $150 per course. For many part-time students, grad school includes other costs, such as travel or baby-sitting, which can be considerable.

Most part-time graduate students cover all costs themselves. Of the students involved in the 1993 NPSAS, only 28% received financial support of any kind. Of that group, 8% took out loans, and 9% received assistance from their employers. Federal, state, and institutional support for part-time master's candidates was—and is—minuscule.

Because financial policies and considerations are crucial to both students and institutions, it is important to carefully consider all the angles, beginning with variables in pricing, both among universities and within them. Search for grants and other forms of direct financial

TABLE 6.2 Average Annual Expenses for Part-Time, Part-Year, or Both Types of Master's Students, by Type of Expense and Institution: 1992 to 1993

College Type	Total Costs	Tuition and Fees	Total Nontuition Expenses	Other Household Expenses While Enrolled	Attendance Costs (by Dollar Amount)
Public	8,644	1,613	7,064	6,315	708
4-year non-doctorate-granting	7,488	929	6,583	5,937	663
4-year doctorate-granting	9,334	2,015	7,352	6,540	736
Private, not for profit	10,743	3,365	7,352	6,553	698
4-year non-doctorate-granting	9,027	2,377	6,626	6,015	651
4-year doctorate granting	11,698	3,904	7,714	6,847	724

Source: U.S. Department of Education, National Center for Education Statistics (1995).

aid. Consider strategies for borrowing money, if necessary. Check out the possibility of reimbursement by your employer as well as the accompanying income tax implications. Although all of these avenues are low-percentage options, it is worth checking them out. If you should locate a source of financial assistance, the reward would fully justify your efforts.

FINDING THE ANGLES

Cost will surely be a consideration as you weigh trade-offs and make your choice of programs. Once you commit to a program, start making every effort to minimize expenses.

As noted in Chapter 2, it is important to make use of every possible transfer hour. Every course, every hour of credit you do not have to take can translate into considerable savings. Because of a tuition system that rewards full-time attendance, a single one-hour course is often financially inconsequential to students carrying a full load. But it can mean serious money to the part-timer. Talk this over with your adviser. If a seemingly unrelated course from an earlier try at grad school can be worked in as an elective, do so. This is especially critical for education students.

Check out even questionable credits. If you took a course or courses so long ago that they might exceed the total time limit, or if you took hours at another institution that exceed the transfer limit, or if you took more hours than you should have before your formal admission, ask your adviser about the possibility of a waiver. Advisers are generally reasonable people; although committed to the integrity of their programs, most like to help students. It will be up to you to explain just why any debatable courses would logically complement your program. But if you can make a good case, you might just succeed.

Try a long shot. Check out the possibility of any deals or discounts in tuition. If you have chosen a public institution, the only variations will be whether you must pay in-state or out-of-state tuition. Sometimes, as noted in Chapter 5, it is possible to avoid out-of-state tuition by enrolling for a very low number of hours each term. Five or fewer semester hours is a limit that is not uncommon. Depending on your program and your plans, this might suit you well.

Your state may have reciprocity arrangements with neighboring states. That is, each state agrees to waive out-of-state tuition for students from the other state.

In some cases, public universities have made unilateral deals to attract out-of-state students. If you are interested in a program offered by a university in a neighboring state, ask about reciprocity and in-state status. Do not wait for the school to raise the subject.

Private colleges and universities normally charge higher tuition rates than public schools. However, because they are not under governmental control, they have the flexibility to charge whatever their trustees will allow. Sometimes, to compete with public schools, they will adjust their tuition rates. Creighton University, in Omaha, for example, offers a 50% tuition reduction—for one course per semester—to teachers and school administrators "who are employed full-time in public or private elementary schools."

FINANCIAL AID

Financial aid of the type provided for undergraduate students does not exist at the graduate level. Such direct aid is a tough sell, politically. Many members of Congress, and the people they represent, believe that the people who benefit from graduate education should be the ones who pay for it. Most federal aid to graduate students is indirect, such as funding to hire graduate assistants in research grants and contracts.

And for the limited federal aid that does exist, part-time students find themselves largely excluded. The Twentieth Century Fund recently assembled a Task Force on Retraining America's Workforce. The task force criticized this bias against part-time study and recommended that the federal government expand the eligibility guidelines for postsecondary financial aid programs—graduate as well as undergraduate—so that more working people could qualify (Florio, 1996). Given the current pressures on Congress and the President to balance the national budget, prospects for such changes seem dim.

▓ Collegiate and Departmental Aid

Universities allocate a portion of their budgets to support graduate students. The greatest part of this aid is administered through the graduate college and, more directly, by academic departments, largely for the purpose of supporting teaching and research assistants. This system puts part-time professional master's students at a double disadvantage. Not only does most assistance of this type go to full-time students, almost all of it is reserved for doctoral candidates.

Harvard, for example, states in its catalog that master's students are ineligible to receive aid from the university. Although usually not stated so explicitly, this policy applies, de facto, in many U.S. universities. Peters (1992) cites a Stanford professor who explained that his department considered tuition from master's students a major source of financial support for the PhD program. Again, this is never a matter of stated policy, of course, but it does describe reality in many graduate programs.

There is nothing sinister about this. Universities must have teaching and research assistants to carry out their missions. Furthermore, part-time students with full-time jobs have no time and little inclination to work in assistantships. In fact, programs that require students to teach or lead lab sections have the effect of excluding part-timers.

Occasionally, academic departments or programs and continuing education offices earmark or dedicate funds to support so-called nontraditional students. This vague term generally includes people beyond traditional college age who are just beginning college, people who dropped out of college and are returning after a period of years, or employed, part-time adult students. Where such funding exists, the levels are quite modest. For example, awards may be limited to tuition for a single course, with no guarantee of renewal from term to term. Other programs may be limited to as few as one student for the course of his or her degree program. That is, when one recipient of the award graduates or otherwise leaves the program, another student is selected. But no matter how limited the award or how tough the competition, apply whenever they are available. If you should receive no more than one term's tuition, one time, the financial savings to your family's treasury will have been significant.

The departments, programs, and offices that control such awards generally do not publicize them widely. Therefore, as you enter a program, do not limit your inquiries to the financial aid office. Ask advisers—both academic and professional—program coordinators, and, yes, departmental secretaries.

▓ Scholarships and Grants

The best money, of course, is "free" money, scholarships or grants that do not have to be paid back. Obviously, the odds against finding free money are long. Nonetheless, it is worth your time to find several of the commercial guides to financing graduate study and examine them carefully. Most are trade paperbacks, available in good bookstores, but some are accessible through the Internet. Several useful sources are listed in Appendix D.

These reference works, whether in print or on the World Wide Web, are updated frequently. Because they are oriented toward full-time study, examining them and teasing out sources of funding appropriate to your circumstances may be laborious. And it might not pay off. However, if you are fortunate, you might find one or more highly specific scholarship or grant opportunities aimed at working professionals.

The National Restaurant Association, for example, offers the Heinz Graduate Degree Fellowship "to present or previous full-time teachers or administrators of food service career education" (Peterson's, 1995, p. 290). The Dietrich, Cross, and Hanley Memorial Scholarships, awarded by the Association of Former Agents of the U.S. Secret Service, are given at the graduate level to help defray the cost of pursuing or furthering careers in law enforcement, with applications from persons currently working in the field encouraged (Peterson's, 1995, p. 111).

Several organizations award grants that can further the careers of working women. The American Association of University Women makes awards "to update course work toward employment goals" (Peterson's, p. 35). The Avon Products Foundation Program for Women in Business Studies is awarded to women seeking an education to enter or reenter business-oriented fields (Peterson's, 1995, pp. 126-127).

As you examine the reference books and databases, look for entries that match your interests and occupation. Sometimes, work experience in a given field is considered a qualification. If you are a woman or qualify as a member of a minority group, examine the appropriate special-interest funding sources. A few scholarships and grants are allocated according to religious affiliation, so check potential denominational sources.

LOANS

Because financial aid programs and departmental fellowships and assistantships are slanted toward doctoral study, full-time master's students often must turn to federal loan programs—the Stafford or Ford programs for schools that participate in the Federal Direct Loan Program, and the Federal Family Education Loan Program for those that do not.

Currently, full-time master's students are piling up fearsome debts, often greater than those incurred by PhD candidates. According to recent studies, borrowing for graduate school is at an all-time high and growing rapidly (Johnson, 1996). On the other hand, only about 8% of working, part-time master's students borrow from student loan programs (USDE, 1995). Thus, the cost of full-time study at the master's level is not only great but long-term. Here, for once, you—as a part-time student—should have a distinct edge. It will take you longer to finish, and you are likely to get little help along the way, but you will probably graduate debt free, or close to it.

Federal student loan programs fall into two categories, subsidized and unsubsidized. In the case of subsidized loans, the government makes the interest payments until the student graduates or leaves school. To receive such loans, the student must establish need. With unsubsidized loans, the recipient must begin making interest payments immediately but is not required to establish need.

Because of their incomes and relatively light course loads, fully employed graduate students rarely qualify for subsidized loans. Income aside, a student must take at least a half-time load to receive a subsidized loan. For unsubsidized federal loans, although the recipient is not required to establish financial need, he or she must nonetheless fill out the same application forms and make the same disclosures about income and resources as students applying for need-based assistance. Last, all direct federal loans include a 4% origination fee. Information about federal programs is available from the financial aid offices of all colleges and universities.

The immediate interest payments, the intrusive application process, the origination fee, and the prospect of a large debt load generally make federal loan programs unattractive to part-time, employed students. Most prefer to avoid long-term credit, if at all possible. Sometimes, however, short-term credit can be helpful.

Tuition, books, and ancillary expenses each semester or quarter can represent an impossible hit on the monthly household cash flow. Many students need to spread that expense over several months but with the intent of paying it off before the next term begins. The best way to handle this situation, of course, is to budget for it in advance. But that is not always possible.

Most universities demand full payment on enrollment each term. Some, however, allow students to spread their tuition payments across the term. At The University of Iowa, for example, students may choose to divide their tuition into several payments. However, there is a $30 charge for this service each term. Many schools and most bookstores allow students to pay by credit card, and many students do so. However, given the high rate of interest on bank credit cards, it is probably best to avoid this option. An approved line of credit from your bank or credit union, if you could qualify, would cost much less, particularly if you should ever find it necessary to carry a balance over more than one term.

EMPLOYER SUPPORT

A minority of U.S. employers provide financial support for graduate-level education. According to the NPSAS (USDE, 1993), only 9% of part-time master's degree students received assistance of any kind from their employers. The Twentieth Century Fund Task Force on Retraining America's Workforce attributed this lack of involvement to a concern on the part of many companies that although employee education might benefit the company, it was more likely that staff would move on, using their new knowledge and skills on behalf of another company (Florio, 1996).

Them That Has, Gets

It is one of the many ironies of graduate study that when employers provide assistance, the greatest amount of aid goes to the better-paid employee. In 1993, 16% of part-time master's students with incomes of more than $50,000 received funding of some sort from their employers, as compared with 9% of those with incomes between $30,000 and $49,999, and only 6% of those earning between $20,000 and $29,999. Part-time master's students who did receive aid were awarded an average of $2,200.

Engineers, managers, and other corporate employees are most likely to receive substantial financial support from their employers. Nurses, teachers, and social workers are usually on their own. Obviously, the former groups normally have much higher average incomes than the latter groups. This phenomenon tells us a great deal about how society values the various professions. When private employers encourage advanced study, they usually do so with the carrot of tuition support. Public employers, on the other hand, are more likely to use the stick of mandated study. Remember also that some private employers, particularly engineering firms, use tuition support for graduate work as a recruiting tool.

Firms that employ human relations development specialists seem to be a special case. In a 1994 survey of 960 human relations professionals, 76% reported that their firms provided tuition reimbursement for employees (Flynn, 1994).

University and college employees make up a separate category. In many cases, their employers can simply waive tuition or dedicate some scholarship funds to staff members, thus providing significant help at essentially no cost to themselves. Although in most cases assistance is restricted to use at the employing school, that is not always the case. For example, the Vermont Law School offers a maximum of $250 on completion of a semester of college work. On receipt of the degree, the employee receives an additional $300. Under this plan, there is an overall maximum of $2,500 per staff member.

▓ Claiming Support

Companies vary in the ways they pay employee tuition support. Alcoa pays full tuition for approved courses at the beginning of each term; employees do not have to put out their own money in advance. Reimbursement after the fact is more common. Many corporations require employees to make an initial commitment of their own funds. Land's End will reimburse tuition up to $1,100 per year (DesMareau, 1995). HAL Computer Systems, which typically hires engineers and computer scientists, will reimburse not only tuition expenses but books and ancillary fees as well, up to $5,000 per year. Sometimes, reimbursement depends on how well students do in their course work. Keane, Inc., a software services company, allocates reimbursement, up to 100%, according to each employee's grades.

Employers often set additional stipulations. Some require courses to be "job-related" to qualify for reimbursement. The meaning of this term varies greatly from company to company. Other companies require students to be accepted into a degree program and to progress at a specified pace. If your employer offers tuition support or reimbursement, check out the terms and stipulations very carefully.

▓ Hidden Subsidies

Whether or not your employer provides direct tuition support to employees, it may subsidize graduate education in other ways. Many graduate programs, especially those offered in the workplace, are the result of partnerships between universities and corporations. Such programs are almost always run on a cost-recovery basis. That means that the offering university must make enough money in tuition and other funds to pay all delivery expenses. This usually includes "overload" pay for the faculty, for whom teaching off-campus or via distance education represents a workload beyond their usual assignments. Frequently, the amount of tuition collected is insufficient to cover all expenses. In such cases, the employer and the school usually have a contractual arrangement by which the former covers costs beyond tuition revenues. Thus, if you are fortunate enough to have a program delivered to your workplace, your employer is probably paying a subsidy above and beyond any direct tuition aid.

The Tax Man Cometh

A recent change in the tax laws has lessened the attractiveness and utility of employer assistance. Congress has long exhibited an ambivalence about using the Internal Revenue Code to promote college attendance by working students, particularly those at the graduate level. Specifically, lawmakers have wavered on the question of whether tuition assistance from employers should or should not be excluded from an individual's taxable income. Noah Brown (1996), Director of Governmental Affairs of the University Continuing Education Association, traced developments leading up to the current situation in a recent article.

Until 1978, working students could exclude employer assistance from their gross income only if college courses were "job-related" under Internal Revenue Service definitions. In practice, the job-related criterion proved both difficult to administer and clearly inequitable. The legal definitions favored employees with the broadest job descriptions, who frequently held positions at the highest income levels. For example, corporate managers had wide latitude in determining job-relatedness, whereas nurses had to meet a much more specific and limited standard. Congress eliminated this distinction with the Employee Educational Assistance Act of 1978, Section 127 of the Internal Revenue Code. Working students could finally exclude employer support for all college courses—at both the graduate and undergraduate levels—from their gross income. According to Brown (1996), this change "contributed to upward mobility by allowing employees to improve their credentials without incurring higher taxes" (p. 18).

To many congresspersons and senators, however, favorable treatment of college-level assistance remained suspicious. Such favoritism would profit employees who already earned the highest salaries. A 1989 Coopers and Lybrand survey appeared to refute this notion. It reported that 99% of those who reported Section 127 benefits had earned less than $50,000 annually, and 71% had earned less than $30,000. Still, Congress remained ambivalent, renewing Section 127 for only a few years at a time and letting it expire temporarily several times (Brown, 1996).

In its most recent battle over Section 127, Congress reinstated it for the period covering 1995 to 1997, but only for undergraduate courses. Thus, employer reimbursement for graduate study is now regarded as taxable income. According to an estimate of the College and University Personnel Association, the change in the law will mean that an unmarried taxpayer who earns $35,000 annually, and who receives $3,000 in employer-provided tuition support, will add another $1,249 to his or her tax load (Brown, 1996).

Although the current status of affairs is certainly not optimal, in most cases, employer-provided tuition support should nonetheless remain a net plus. In addition, given the legislative history of Section 127, the recent congressional action should not be taken as final. If your employer has a tuition support plan, keep an eye on future legislative action.

CONCLUSION

As I noted earlier in this chapter, most part-time students—especially those with full-time jobs—receive no financial support at all. However, consider the huge accumulated debts of most full-time students—especially at the master's level—along with the income they have forgone. In comparison, for the person with a good job and a career well under way, part-time study, especially in pursuit of the professional master's degree, makes a good deal of sense, even without any external support at all. The additional time required for part-time students to earn the degree is usually more than offset by the relative lack of debt on graduation, as well as by the accelerated progress in their careers.

REFERENCES

Brown, J. N. (1996, Winter). Congress threatens tax-exempt status of employer-provided tuition assistance. *Educational Record,* 18-19.

DesMareau, K. (1995, August). Learning to win. *Bobbin,* 130-138.

Florio, J. (1996, July 18). Worker training: Serious business for nation's future. *Chicago Tribune,* section 1, p. 11.

Flynn, G. (1994). Career development is a company attention-getter. *Personnel Journal,* *73*(10), 22.

HAL World Wide Web page. (1996).

Johnson, M. (1996, June 28). Debt remains long after graduation. *Daily Iowan,* p. A1.

Keane World Wide Web page. (1996).

Peters, R. L. (1992). *Getting what you came for: The smart student's guide to earning a master's* *or a Ph.D.* New York: Noonday.

Peterson's grants for graduate and postdoctoral study (4th ed.). (1995). Princeton, NJ: Peterson's.

U.S. Department of Education, National Center for Education Statistics. (1995). *1992-1993* *national postsecondary student aid study (NPSAS: 93), graduate data analysis system.* Washington, DC: Author.

7

Almost Human

The heavens themselves, the planets, and this center
Observe degree, priority, and place,
Insistiture, course, proportion, season, form,
Office, and custom, all in line of order.
—Shakespeare, *Troilus and Cressida*

Perhaps the greatest challenge working, adult, part-time graduate students face is observing degree, priority, and place, and keeping them in order. Several of the more unfortunate features of graduate student culture result from an inability to maintain a sense of proportion and priorities. For too many students, divorce and other relationship problems, excessive drinking, despair, procrastination, and other self-defeating behaviors accompany graduate school attendance.

Although these hazards can affect part-time students as well as their full-time counterparts, it has been my experience that the former group is less susceptible. The academic grind, along with immersion in the campus culture, can begin to wear students down, especially those whose identities are totally wrapped up in academic life. Most adult students, on the other hand, accommodate to their new roles fairly quickly. If not, they decide that it will not work, then leave. Few are dismissed.

I am not suggesting that you will not have to make adjustments or convince yourself that you can do it. Indeed, the initial quarter or semester will almost certainly be traumatic. However, if that term goes well, you should have a high probability of success in subsequent academic terms.

It is not unusual for people who begin graduate school several years after earning their bachelor's degrees to feel some trepidation about returning to the campus. Many report feeling like impostors. Colin Powell (Powell, 1995) used this word in describing his feelings as he began work on his MBA at the age of 32—the oldest student in his class—after more than a decade as a career soldier. Like many graduate students who have been away from college for some time, he entered with considerable anxiety about his ability to handle courses, especially those based on quantitative methodology. Yet, after an initial adjustment, he did well in his studies, while keeping his career and family foremost in his priorities.

Many adult students returning to earn graduate degrees actually have a great deal going for them. Like General Powell, they tend to be more grounded in their identities. They are not wrapped in the graduate culture; they realize there is no need to please professors, at least beyond the point of earning good grades. Their futures do not depend on their adviser's connections and influence. And they have a clear, defined sense of priorities.

If you are at the point of entering graduate school to advance your career, you have probably already attained a degree of professional recognition. You have been tested and have succeeded. The graduate education and degree represent the tools and credentials—either necessary or simply useful—to make the next major step. Thus, you should possess a basic confidence in yourself and in your ability, perhaps not specifically as a student but certainly as a professional. Full-time students, especially those proceeding directly from their undergraduate studies, are often confident but sometimes without reason. Their abilities have not yet been tested. And unlike these students, you have probably already learned to juggle several important roles; becoming a student is just one more.

Of course, no new enterprise as momentous as graduate school, especially undertaken while working full-time, will be easy or undemanding. Nor would it be worth the time or money if it were. Grad study will definitely have a major impact on your personal life. You will have to make changes in your life that will affect the lives of the people around you, people whom you love or respect, or both, or at least whose good will you need. They may occasionally find it hard to live with you. And not surprisingly, you may occasionally find it hard to live with yourself.

LIFE WITH YOUR HARSHEST CRITIC

Most people are harder on themselves than anyone else. Certainly, most of us expect a great deal of ourselves. Adding graduate school to already complicated lives can intensify our expectations and our fears. All graduate students have to cope with varying degrees of stress, frustration, anger, and sometimes even depression. But none of these emotions or conditions is unique to graduate school. And again, I would argue that working, part-time students are less troubled by such problems than students who are totally committed to the academic culture. At the very least, working professionals have more experience in performing under pressure and scrutiny.

There can be no doubt that adding graduate study to a busy life will produce additional stress. But we know that stress, in itself, is not harmful. A certain amount of stress is not only acceptable but necessary, to perform well. The critical issue is how we handle it. If handled well, stress can be a positive factor in our lives. If handled badly, it can lead to failure and miserable interactions with other people. None of this is original or even particularly perceptive, of course. Indeed, it is commonplace. Stress is present in any enterprise. The only way to handle it successfully is to recognize it for what it is, then deal with the symptoms as they occur. Walter Gmelch (1993) has written a book, in Sage's "Survival Skills for Scholars" series, called *Coping With Academic Stress*. In it, he deals with aspects of stress—positive as well as negative—particular to the academic life. Even though Gmelch wrote it for a faculty audience, you should find it helpful in dealing with the stress of graduate study and multiple roles.

Stress is one of several factors that can contribute to a more damaging problem, depression. At the risk of becoming overly repetitive and despite a lack of empirical evidence, experience has convinced me that part-time students are less inclined to encounter depression than full-time students. This has to do with the differing importance of school in the lives of each group. To the full-time student who intends to use a graduate degree as the initial springboard to a career, it is everything. To the part-time student, it is important, but it is not everything. In addition, the working student finds it much harder to withdraw from contact and involvement with others—one of the classic symptoms of depression.

Short periods of feeling "down" or "blue" are normal, of course. We all have them. You will experience them whether or not you are in school. However, if you should have trouble bouncing back from such episodes, it might be a good idea to check with your doctor. Although depression can be devastating, it is also imminently treatable for most people. Certainly if you have a history of depression, it would be a good idea to discuss your plans for graduate school with your doctor as you begin your program.

More common than depression are simple anger and frustration, directed either toward the classroom situation, as discussed in Chapter 4, or the administrative end of grad school described in Chapter 5. And these emotions can be particularly troublesome, or at least surprising, to working, part-time students who, as Selke and Wong (1993) noted, "are successful, experienced adults who are more accustomed to giving advice than to receiving it" (p. 21).

Anger over bureaucratic snarls or antiquated graduate college rules is rarely productive. Letting that anger linger and become an ongoing sense of frustration can be destructive. Dealing with anger in short order is absolutely necessary. However, this can be tricky. On the one hand, you do not want to surrender your autonomy and constantly give in to people no smarter than yourself. Developing a feeling of dependence on the institution and the people who run it is one of the real dangers of graduate school. If you allow yourself to be treated like a child, you could become childlike. This is one of the rarely discussed hazards of the academic culture. On the other hand, most slights and offenses on the school's part are unintentional and impersonal. Some of them even make sense once you make an effort to understand them. Also, do not mistake incompetence or indifference—which exist in universities as they do in all workplaces—for maliciousness. If you contest every minor slight or offense, you can work yourself into a perpetual state of outrage. It isn't worth it.

Do not be afraid to question either the academic or administrative people you will encounter, but do not become a pest. There is no quicker way to make people stop paying attention to your complaints. The best course of action probably is to pick your spots carefully. Most of the time it is probably best to tell yourself, "it's all part of the harassment," shrug it off, and go on. However, sometimes you may find it necessary to assert your autonomy and demand to be treated as an intelligent adult. As such, you are capable of sorting out the screw-ups from the serious offenses. Either way, do what you must do, then let go. Carrying a grudge is a particularly unproductive course of behavior.

The degree of stress-related difficulties you may face will depend to a great extent on the pace you have selected. If you take only one course at a time, you may find the road less than arduous. If you take two courses, the demands may become more frantic and the way more difficult. If you should take more than two courses while holding down a full-time job, you will almost certainly find yourself overwhelmed. And even within these options, the workload will vary widely. Some semesters or quarters will be worse than others. Some professors will be a joy, some mildly boring, and some dreadful. But every grad student, full-time or part-time, encounters this. In a sense, this is a measure of equality between resident, full-time students and working adults. You, like they, will see the best and the worst the university has to offer.

Sometimes, students who do well in the prescribed course work of a master's degree program experience difficulty when they reach the relatively unstructured requirements—the practicum, an independent study course, a thesis or project, or study for the comprehensive examinations. After the earlier externally imposed discipline, the relative freedom of working on one's own can be daunting. Sadly, there is no trick to make this kind of work easy. Self-discipline, literally forcing yourself to proceed, is the only answer. The good news is that if you have not yet developed the habit of controlling your own workload, the exercise of doing so will serve you well long after graduation.

Assuming that you have a heavy but manageable workload, the best way of managing stress and avoiding depression is to keep on keeping on. As Peters (1992) said in his excellent book on coping with graduate school, *Getting What You Came For,* "daily progress is the best antidote for procrastination depression" (p. 129). Peters is right; for a student, procrastination is both a cause and a symptom of depression. Avoiding procrastination is by far the most effective means of preventing depression.

Avoiding procrastination is a long-term as well as short-term process. An overall timetable is essential, both as a guide to staying on track and as a reminder that the process will end. One student studying for a master's in adult and continuing education at George Washington University, while working full-time at the same institution, put it this way, "It's like scheduling your life; 'In three years,' you've got to tell yourself, 'I want to be finished with this and finished with that' " (Taylor, 1993, p. 24). She was right. If you fall into the habit of looking at school as an endless grind, it will be easy to fall into a funk.

Accept reality. Something will have to go. When you add the rigor of grad school to your life, you cannot continue to do everything you have been doing. One determined and experienced part-time doctoral student, who had also earned his bachelor's and master's degrees while working full time, described his decision to give up model railroading and fishing for the duration of his studies: "It's pretty tough, but you [need] balance, and you have to let some things go, and those are leisure activities" (Taylor, 1993, p. 23).

Because these are the types of activities people normally take up to reduce stress and add enjoyment to life, giving them up can be hard; life may suddenly seem more grim. You will have to make the adjustments, but perhaps it will not be necessary to give up your favorite activities entirely. Perhaps you can play tennis or bowl once a week, often enough to keep you in the game but not enough to become a major distraction. Or you may find it best just to put some activities on hold. Perhaps you can let the garden go for a couple of years or take an unofficial leave of absence from service clubs.

Although you can't avoid cutting back your other activities, it would be a mistake to use school as an excuse to give up things that are an important part of your life. For example, I hate to exercise. I know it is good for me, but I can't learn to like it. Although it is an unpleasant part of my life, unfortunately, it is an important one. Throughout graduate school, I had to fight the temptation to use my schedule and workload as excuses to skip it or to quit it altogether. On another level, if taking your family to worship services is a fixture in your lives, you should probably continue to do so, perhaps cutting out such ancillary activities as committee meetings and social functions. You will have to make numerous decisions about which activities are critical to your life and family and which are simply pleasant and enjoyable.

Last, there will be some less than vital things you just will not quite make yourself give up. When that happens, the trick is to keep them in proportion. Let's say you are a devoted Chicago Bears fan. Of course you are going to watch them play the Minnesota Vikings on television. However, it is important that you not remain in front of the television when that game ends and the late game comes on, featuring two teams from California you care nothing about. Then it is time to turn off the set and open the books.

Coming to grips with the way graduate school will change your lifestyle can be tough. Depending on the school you selected, you may be eligible for free counseling. Or another way to look at it is that you may be forced to pay for it, whether you use it or not, through your student activities or health fees. Unfortunately, some schools continue to maintain daytime hours only for these services, making them impractical for part-time students, despite the fact that they are enrolling growing numbers of working people.

The point is, if you think counseling could help, it is a good idea to seek it, whether or not it is available through your school. If you can use university services, be sure to do so. Although adult students are often reluctant to use these services, you should not be. If you are paying for the services, you are entitled to use them.

If you are concerned about your adjustment to grad school but do not think formal counseling is necessary, you might want to see your general or family practitioner or clergy member. If you are not ready for even that, at least talk out the situation with your spouse, partner, or a good friend. Then if you still need to step up to the next level, do so.

In *Getting What You Came For,* Peters (1992) has some wise words about the last resort. He wrote them for the full-time student, but his message is perhaps even more applicable for part-timers, especially those with full-time jobs and families. You may need to quit.

If you cannot gear up academically within a term or two, if you are unable to adjust your schedule to your new commitments, if your spouse or partner cannot manage to be supportive, and if the pressure does not ease off, you probably need to consider giving it up. Sometimes, the best way to deal with pressure is to remove its source. To retreat to the controlling cliché of this book, graduate school creates a constant series of trade-offs. If you should decide that the degree is not worth the sacrifices it demands, leaving would be the best course of action for yourself and those around you. There is no profit in investing energy, emotion, time, and money in something that makes you miserable.

You probably will not have to agonize over this. It has been my experience that most part-time graduate students decide quickly that they will succeed and earn the degree or that they do not belong in school.

KEEPING YOUR
FAMILY ON YOUR SIDE

Elizabeth Hill (1995), a veteran adviser of adult, part-time students who has written extensively on advising this population, recalled one adult student considering graduate school who told her, "I know what classes I'll need to take. What I want for you to tell me is what's going to happen to my marriage" (p. 124). That student already understood something of critical importance. He was contemplating a course of action that would have a profound—and possibly destructive—impact not just on himself but on those he lived with.

Part-time study will change the dynamics of a marriage or marriagelike partnership. In a real partnership, the division of labor will change. The partner not going to school may have to spend more time driving and supervising the kids, for example. If a couple cannot make such common adjustments, however, their relationship is probably already shaky. But the changes could be considerably more challenging. All the members of a family or relationship might have to accept major lifestyle changes.

It is necessary, I believe, to bring all of the family members into the process before you make a final decision. Explain to them in as much detail as they would like what you are considering doing and why. Tell them how you think this new demand on your time and energy will affect your life and theirs, both short-term and long-range. Ask about their concerns and consider them seriously.

Such discussions must run on two levels, of course. Kids cannot have an equal vote when their parents make major decisions. Still, they need to be consulted and treated seriously and respectfully. Your spouse or partner's vote is another matter. If the two of you cannot come to a wholehearted agreement, you have a major problem. You may need to reconsider your plans.

Most of the time, families are initially supportive. They understand that the advanced degree is intended to benefit not only the person taking it but themselves as well. As time goes on, however, and the burden of housework and baby-sitting remains one-sided, vacations are limited or skipped, and parties and children's occasions are missed, their enthusiasm may wane. You may begin to notice some resentment. And, especially if you have small children, you will probably feel some guilt.

In some extreme cases, married adult students may experience resentment so extreme as to constitute sabotage. The mate or partner who is not going to school can grow to resent the one who is. From admittedly anecdotal evidence I have received from the programs I have worked with, from the experience of advisers of adult students I have known, and from colleagues who work at other institutions, this kind of disruptive behavior does, in fact, occur. Undergraduate women students are most often—but not always—the targets.

Years ago, when I first started hearing about this kind of occurrence, I thought the stories were probably exaggerated, that such incidents would be highly unlikely at the graduate level. Then, a friend actually encountered such a situation. She was working on a graduate degree in nursing while holding a full-time hospital job. Near the end of a semester, as she was completing a major paper and beginning to study for finals, her husband—a PhD himself—walked into the house with a "surprise," tickets for a long weekend at a resort in Arizona. He said that he knew she had been working hard and needed a break. Also, the trip fit in with his schedule. Because he had already purchased the tickets and made reservations, she felt she had no choice but to go, which of course added even more pressure at the end of the term, which he had obviously intended. In another, more overt case that occurred in a higher education program I taught in, a wife openly and persistently made her husband's life miserable for the duration of his studies. Somehow, he persisted and earned his degree. I do not know what happened to the marriage.

You probably will not face anything this drastic. However, if your family life becomes a constant state of tension, you must deal with it right away. If talking it out does not work, counseling might help.

In most cases, you and the people you live with will learn to deal with the day-to-day annoyances and misunderstandings that are part of life in any family. Rely on your common sense. Try to remain sensitive to the feelings of your family or partner, keep communications open, deal with problems as they come up, and give what time you can. Keep the long view in mind. You probably would not be making the sacrifices necessary to attend graduate school unless you believed that it would improve their lives as well as your own.

The problem of reconciling graduate study with your family or relationship is not only a long-range matter. It will come up every term, as you decide which and how many courses you will take. Perhaps you could do fine with one course, but because of quirks in your school's schedule, you really need to take two classes in a given semester. Or perhaps everything worked fine when you had classes on a Monday night, but when you had to take a particular class on Wednesday night, it began to interfere with your spouse's plans.

Take every opportunity you can to spend time with the people close to you. As you plan the chores and divide labor, try to work with somebody. Sort the laundry or cook with your spouse. Wash the car and rake leaves with your kids. Make a real effort to talk, and really listen, as you work.

Perhaps you can plan activities so that you can solve several problems at once. For example, perhaps your spouse is in the habit of going out on the same night each week to bowl or attend investment club meetings. You can start the kids on their homework, then get busy on your own. Spend a little time with them as they finish their work, then let them goof off for a while as you resume your work. Then put them to bed and get back to work. In such a case, not only did your spouse get a night out of the house, but you were a presence in your children's lives. Even though you were reading or writing, you were nonetheless there. Although you may have had to work in short bursts between interruptions, you did work. Besides, you probably work between constant phone calls and other interruptions on the job. Working adults are often very good at this.

If you have children, it is possible that there may be something in it for them when you become a university student. Perhaps they will be eligible to use its recreational facilities. Or perhaps you might like the pleasure of introducing your teenager to a first-rate library.

Nobody can be perpetually "on." Even the busiest, most well-organized people waste a little time. But it is possible to waste time wisely. For example, when I was a graduate student, I found that I simply could not do any productive work on Friday nights. I could spend Saturday and Sunday in the library, but on Friday nights, I was useless. It was therefore better to write them off, enjoy them, and then get to work on Saturday morning. If there is such a time slot in your life, make a point of using it to take your spouse to dinner or a movie or to play with your kids. Then, you can feel considerably less guilty when you isolate yourself to work on a paper all day Saturday.

As a working professional, you have already learned the value of organization in your work. It is also the key when integrating your new role as a student into your ongoing role as a spouse, partner, and/or parent. You are probably already using a calendar or organizer of some sort on the job. All of the organizing tools, despite their individual features, essentially rest on making out daily and weekly schedules, setting priorities, and making lists and sticking to them, although leaving some flexibility to allow for response to unexpected or urgent situations and opportunities. Adapt your calendar or organizer to coordinate all of your roles. Treat your daughter's piano recital and your statistics exam just as you would a meeting with your principal or the head of the sales division.

During the latter part of my grad student days at the University of Georgia, several of us noticed how extraordinarily efficient one of our classmates was. She held a responsible job, had a family, and did wonderful work in our course. Unlike the rest of us, however, she never complained; she never seemed rushed or stressed. Naturally, we wanted to know how she did it. She said that every Sunday night, she spent about 15 minutes carefully planning the upcoming week. She made a master list and schedule that she then lived by.

"If I don't put something on the list, it does not get done, period," she said. "But you have to keep it in perspective." She told us about one Sunday night when she noticed that her husband was taking an unusual interest as she made out her weekly schedule and list. He pointedly asked her, twice, if she had written down *everything*. She finally caught on, opened her organizer and made a couple more entries. Thereafter, it became a weekly joke—and ritual—as she organized her calendar, for her husband to ask if she had listed *everything*.

Although schedules and lists are necessary to effectively coordinate at least three distinct roles, it is possible to take them too far, as my classmate did. You will not want your family to think that they are not entitled to your time and attention unless you have "penciled them in." Family life, much more than our work or school lives, takes place on an impromptu basis. Organization, although essential, has its limits. If you have small kids, they will interrupt you. This is a given. But try not to use such interruptions as an excuse for putting your books aside for an hour or for an evening. You probably cope with constant interruptions at work and still keep going. You can do so when studying statistics or psychology.

No matter how careful you are, your status as a student will demand sacrifices on the part of your family. You will probably make both short-term and long-term efforts to compensate for this. However, do not overdo feelings of guilt. "Sacrifice" is not synonymous with "deprivation." You have their welfare in mind as well as your own. Besides, if you have children, you will be serving as a good example, teaching them about the value of hard work, persistence, and deferred gratification.

YOUR COLLEAGUES AND FRIENDS

If you are typical of the people who begin part-time graduate study, work probably was the most important reason. If a graduate degree is more or less an expectation of your employer, your enrollment should not represent a threat to your colleagues. You are probably not the first of your peers to take on the role of part-time student. Therefore, in most cases, your status as a graduate student should be compatible with the culture of your workplace.

If your office, school district, or squadron often has people in class, it should be expected that you will need a little slack from time to time. This might be a day off to study for finals or an understanding that you may rearrange your schedule so that you can get to class on time. Or, someone else might be asked to make a sudden out-of-town troubleshooting trip in your stead. Thus, even in the best of workplace situations, your participation in graduate school could create some inconvenience for your supervisor or manager or your coworkers. You will need their good will. Therefore, it would be a bad idea to take their acquiescence for granted.

If a school-related absence on your part should inconvenience someone, apologize. If someone goes out of his or her way to help cover for you, be sure to thank that person. When this happens frequently, it is important to let the people involved know that you sincerely appreciate their help. An occasional card, flowers, bottle of wine, or pack of golf balls would acknowledge their help and your continued appreciation. In a good workplace, people should not mind helping each other. But they deserve thanks. And when you complete your degree, it would be appropriate to return the favor, both to the people who helped you and to employees who are just beginning their degree work.

In an organization in which graduate education is part of the culture, success is generally an expectation. This can be a strong motivational factor. On the other hand, it can intensify the pressure and create a fear of failure. If this should happen, and if it should persist, it could upset your relationship with your colleagues. Should the pressure start to get to you, deal with it quickly. You cannot afford to create and reinforce ill will among your coworkers. In extreme cases, it might be necessary to leave school. As with your family, giving up school should be preferable to ruining your career and alienating the people you must work with. At the very least, it would be a good idea to talk out the implications with your company's personnel office. At the risk of sounding like Ann Landers again, counseling might be helpful. But whatever actions you choose, you cannot ignore the problem.

Up to this point, I have assumed that you are working in an environment in which support for graduate education by employees is either a matter of formal policy or strong informal consensus. But this is not the case everywhere. For example, although a school district might expect teachers to earn a master's degree, this expectation might have little impact within a given school building. The other teachers, even those making desultory progress toward a degree, might resent the one or two of you who are making real progress, perhaps even viewing you as threats. Or sometimes, when it seems clear that an advanced degree is going to move a teacher into administration, jealousy becomes a factor.

Such circumstances and feelings are not limited to teachers. In any organization, the realization that a person is about to use a graduate degree to make a major career step, and therefore will soon be elevated above his or her peers, can cause hard feelings.

If you should find yourself in an unsupportive—or even hostile—workplace situation, the going will obviously be much tougher. You will need to ask for as few favors or accommodations as possible, while maintaining your usual productivity. It would also be advisable not to annoy your colleagues by complaining about how busy you are.

Maintaining good friendships while adding a rigorous study schedule to the usual complications of life can be even trickier than getting along with your colleagues. One of the saddest of all the trade-offs associated with part-time graduate study is that a person ordinarily does lose some friends. There is simply not as much time to invest in them once classes and study get underway. This is particularly true for friendships based on activities, such as tennis, bowling, bridge or poker, or community theater. Beyond that, it is common for a person's interests to change as a result of his or her studies.

It is likely that you will make new friends among your fellow students, due to your mutual interest in finance, counseling, information systems, or whatever else you have chosen to study. But remember to keep this in perspective. Drifting apart from some old friends and making new ones is not unique to attending graduate school. It is a continuation of a normal pattern in our lives. We tend to lose touch with old friends from college or the military. When our kids are small, we tend to make friends of some of the parents of their friends. But we ordinarily see these people less and less as our children grow up. Thus, friendships change throughout our lives. In that respect, graduate school is no more disruptive of friendships than many other parts of our lives.

A FINAL TIP

An ability to keep the various facets of your life organized, a sense of perspective and priorities, consideration for those around you, and a commitment to maintaining their good will are all keys to remaining almost human during your pursuit of a graduate degree. But there is one more habit you can develop to avoid alienating your family, colleagues, and friends, and even yourself. Do not allow yourself to become self-absorbed.

Many graduate students, both full-time and part-time, get into the habit of talking about their studies incessantly, as if everyone was as interested as they in secondary curriculum or fiscal policy. In particular, they tend to exaggerate the importance of their studies, boring friends with the details of their reading and research. In my opinion, students pick up this bad habit from professors, a group for which self-absorption is an occupational hazard. Face it; most people are not interested when you tell them, "I'm working on an important study of comparative desktop heights in secondary schools in Iowa's Linn and Muscatine Counties."

Even worse, many graduate students—again, like professors—get into the habit of constant whining about how busy they are. For grad students, this habit is normally temporary. Unlike the faculty, they usually get over it following graduation. But while it lasts, it can be infuriating to its victims. If you can avoid this bad habit of self-centered conversation featuring laments about your overwhelming workload, you stand a better chance of graduating with your family intact and your other relationships on a sound footing. And best of all, no one will mistake you for a professor.

REFERENCES

Gmelch, W. (1993). *Coping with academic stress.* Newbury Park, CA: Sage.

Hill, E. H. (1995). Campus support services in continuing education. In V. W. Mott & C. Rampp (Eds.), *Administration of continuing education* (pp. 115-134). Checotah, OK: AP Publications.

Peters, R. L. (1992). *Getting what you came for: The smart student's guide to earning a master's or a Ph.D.* New York: Noonday.

Powell, C. (with Persico, J.). (1995). *My American journey.* New York: Ballantine.

Selke, M. F., & Wong, T. D. (1993). The mentoring-empowered model: Professional role functions in graduate student advisement. *NACADA Journal, 13*(2), 21-26.

Taylor, V. (1993, July 15). Part-time grad students feel the social and academic pinch. *Black Issues in Higher Education,* 22-24.

THE CURVE IS UP

*Knowledge of what is possible
is the beginning of happiness.*
—George Santayana

Throughout this book, I have occasionally criticized some universities for their limited receptivity to part-time graduate students. And indeed, when a bureaucracy has been designed to serve one model of graduate study—the full-time, resident doctoral candidate—it can seem inefficient and unresponsive, if not hostile or indifferent, to students with a different agenda. Despite the fact that most graduate students attend part-time and far more are pursuing master's degrees than doctorates, the research-driven PhD model still has a disproportionate influence on the way many—but certainly not all—universities conduct their professional master's programs. Although institutions may even realize that there is a "new paradigm," as Glazer (1986, p. 3) posited, day-to-day administration has not caught up with this reality in many cases. Constraints associated with the old paradigm live on. Many schools have been especially slow to make their policies, regulations, and services more user-friendly to the working adult, part-time student population.

My criticism, however, has been limited to matters of administration and the culture of the academy. In properly accredited U.S. universities, there is no problem with the quality of master's degree curriculums. Indeed, U.S. graduate education is the envy of the world, as evidenced by the number of international students who seek it out. Overall, U.S. universities have changed or enlarged their curricula to meet the new paradigm of the professional degree.

Academic currency is far more important than administrative reform to both part-time and full-time students. The quality and utility of the classes and other degree components, and a degree's ultimate value as a professional credential, far outweigh any irritations and annoyances that may accompany it.

There are, in fact, hopeful signs. Overall, conditions are rapidly improving for working women and men interested in part-time graduate study, particularly for those seeking a professional credential. Part-time graduate study is already a buyer's market and is becoming ever more student-customer driven. Although comprehensive, research-based universities are moving more slowly than other types of institutions, even they are changing. Like all other types of graduate-degree-offering institutions, they are aggressively seeking part-time, professionally oriented students for their graduate programs.

This may not always be apparent at the institutional level. In some offices, like that of the graduate dean, and in some faculty lounges, an outdated attitude sometimes can still be detected. It rests on a belief that graduate school is for doctoral candidates and that master's programs, at best, are ancillary. Furthermore, according to this mind-set, because the institution's program is superior, good students not only will choose it but will accept whatever conditions are imposed on them.

Even where such an attitude still exists, it is no longer universal. Remember, at most universities, no one is really in charge. Although some people who work there are indifferent to the part-time student, others badly want to create and administer programs to serve that audience. The latter group usually includes such people as the professors and collegiate-level administrators running the executive MBA program, who actively seek students from corporations based in that state, and education college faculty with ties to local school districts. Engineering faculty, who often have ties with local industries and government agencies—based on research and consulting—have been particularly innovative in designing master's programs for their alumni and other members of their profession. And the division of continuing education at any university works hard to drive up enrollments in off-campus programs as well as those delivered via distance education formats.

Beyond large universities, other types of schools covet your presence, and that of people like you, even more openly and aggressively. Urban universities, for example, have long considered that serving working people is part of their mission and have adapted their administrative and faculty schedules to accommodate them. Many private universities have become dependent on part-time programs as a source of discretionary income. Specialized nonprofit and proprietary schools depend on students like you for their very existence.

By almost any measure, at almost any graduate-degree-granting institution, conditions and choices for part-time students are improving. Competition to attract tuition-paying adult students; instructional formats based on new communications technologies; and the sheer force of corporate, governmental, and individual demand for advanced professional credentials are forcing change.

Many postsecondary institutions are rethinking their policies on such matters as residency requirements and transfer credit. They are making such simple but effective changes as expanding the hours of important campus offices and hiring staff specifically to recruit and serve part-time students. As a result, student satisfaction seems to be increasing. Powers and Rossman (1985), for example, found part-time and full-time graduate students in education equally satisfied with program quality. This certainly matches my observations of practice over the past decade.

The graduate faculty members are becoming accustomed to teaching adult students, and this is improving the quality of programs for part-timers. Many professors particularly enjoy the interaction with working professionals. Management professors can learn how frontline managers deal with corporate problems, working nurses bring experiences from their floors to the classroom, and case workers help social work professors keep in touch with their fields. For many professors as well as students, not only is such interaction stimulating, but it can engender mutual affinity and respect. I cannot prove this to be the case, but such faculty satisfaction seems to be a factor as colleges and departments make some of their programs more user-friendly to adult students.

The diversity of options and learning formats is increasing rapidly. Distance education, in particular, is profoundly improving access to graduate study. Qualified students from virtually anywhere in the country may enroll in highly specialized programs, such as that of the College for Financial Planning; programs from premier universities, such as George Washington's Educational Technology Leadership master's degree; and even programs from foreign universities, such as Heriot-Watt's and Athabasca's business administration and education programs.

Both part-time study and distance education are gaining credibility. As noted in Chapter 5, a series of empirical studies that compared part-time and full-time programs and found no significant differences led the Council on Social Work Education to drop its one-year residency requirement. Many universities have waived residency requirements for programs such as MBA's and engineering master's offered at corporate and industrial sites. This practice is definitely spreading.

After initial skepticism, several accrediting associations have begun to accept, and even endorse, distance education for graduate programs. Among the specialized agencies, the American Assembly of Collegiate Schools of Business (AACSB), which accredits the finest MBA programs in the country, the Council on Social Work Education, and the American Library Association are particularly notable in this respect. Among the regional bodies, the North Central Association, the country's largest, is probably the most forward looking. The UOP, for example, has grown to an enrollment of 35,000 by offering professional degree programs to part-time students via off-campus classes and a well-developed, but initially controversial, computer-assisted instructional model. The UOP's president calls the North Central Association's decision to accredit his institution the single most critical factor in its growth and success (Tucker, 1996).

I would be extremely surprised if this tendency on the part of the accrediting agencies to foster innovation in instructional formats were to be reversed. Corporate and student demand will not permit it. The range of formats, and thus of program and institutional choices, should continue to grow.

The final factor in the growing attractiveness of part-time graduate study is the cost. Graduate school, in whatever mode or venue, is not cheap. Unless an employer is willing to pay for it, an advanced degree mandates a considerable financial sacrifice, as noted in Chapter

6. However, if you can earn your degree while working, you will come out far ahead of the person who leaves work for a year or two, forgoes his or her income for that period, and graduates with a huge debt. The part-timer has the advantage in both the long run and short run.

Graduate school is rarely easy. And it should not be. Working it in with a job, a family, and a normal life is challenging. I have not hesitated to point out that it can also be frustrating and occasionally can provoke deep anger. However, even given all of that, it can be both intellectually and professionally challenging and the key to an improved future for you and your family. More institutions would like you to consider them, and this competition, along with advanced technology, is creating more options and better conditions for students. All indicators are positive.

REFERENCES

Glazer, J. (1986). *The master's degree: Tradition, diversity, innovation.* Washington, DC: Association for the Study of Higher Education.

Powers, S., & Rossman, M. H. (1985). Student satisfaction with graduate education: Dimensionality and assessment in a college education. *Psychology, A Quarterly Journal of Human Behavior, 22*(2), 47-49.

Tucker, R. (1996, Summer). From the void: An interview with John Sperling. *Adult Assessment Forum,* 3-7.

APPENDIX A:
REGIONAL AND SPECIALIZED
ACCREDITING AGENCIES

REGIONAL ACCREDITING ASSOCIATIONS

Middle States Association of College and Schools
3624 Market Street
Philadelphia, PA 19104-2680
Ph: 215-662-5606
Fax: 215-662-5501

New England Association of Schools and Colleges
209 Burlington Road
Bedford, MA 01730-1433
Ph: 617-271-0022
Fax: 617-271-0950

North Central Association of Colleges and Schools
159 North Dearborn Street
Chicago, IL 60601
Ph: 312-263-0456, 1-800-621-7440
Fax: 312-263-7462

Northwest Association of Schools and Colleges
Boise State University
1910 University Drive
Boise, ID 83725
Ph: 208-334-3226
Fax: 208-334-3228

Southern Association of Colleges and Schools
1866 Southern Lane
Decatur, GA 30033-4097
Ph: 404-679-4500, 1-800-248-7701
Fax: 404-679-4558

Western Association of Schools and Colleges
533 Airport Boulevard
Suite 200
Burlingame, CA 94010
Ph: 415-375-7711
Fax: 415-375-7790

SELECTED SPECIALIZED ACCREDITING AGENCIES AND HIGHER EDUCATION

■ Associations

Accrediting Board for Engineering and Technology
345 East 47th Street
New York, NY 10017
212-705-7685

Accreditation Bureau of Health Education Schools
Oak Manor Office
29089 US-20 West
Elkhart, IN 46514
219-293-0124

Accrediting Council on Education in Journalism and Mass Communications
Accrediting Committee
University of Kansas

School of Journalism
Lawrence, KS 66045
913-864-3973

American Assembly of Collegiate Schools of Business
Accreditation Council
605 Old Ballas Road, Suite 200
Saint Louis, MO 63141-7077
314-872-8481

American Association of Colleges for Teacher Education
One Dupont Circle, NW
Suite 610
Washington, DC 20036-2412
202-293-2450

American Library Association
Committee on Accreditation
50 Huron Street
Chicago, IL 60611
312-280-2432

American Society for Engineering Education
Eleven Dupont Circle, NW
Suite 200
Washington, DC 20036
202-986-8500

Association of Collegiate Business Schools and Programs
7007 College Boulevard, Suite 420
Overland Park, Kansas 66211
Ph: 913-339-9356
Fax: 913-339-6226

Association of University Programs in Health Administration
1911 North Fort Myer Drive
Suite 503
Arlington, VA 22209
703-524-5500

Computing Sciences Accreditation Board, Inc. (CSAB)
Computer Science Accreditation Commission
Two Landmark Square, Suite 209
Stamford, CT 06901
203-975-1117

Council on Education for Public Health
1015 15th Street, NW
Suite 403
Washington, DC 20005
202-789-1050

Council on Social Work Education
1600 Duke Street
Suite 300
Alexandria, VA 22314
703-683-8080

National Council for Accreditation of Teacher Education
2010 Massachusetts Avenue NW
Suite 200
Washington, DC 20036-1023
202-466-7496

National League for Nursing
350 Hudson Street
New York, NY 10014
212-989-9393

Social Science Education Consortium
3300 Mitchell Lane, Suite 240
Boulder, CO 80301
303-492-8154

Appendix B:
Council of Graduate
Schools Guidelines

Academic Guidelines Policy Statement, Council of Graduate Schools, May 1989. The Council of Graduate Schools recommends the following guidelines for establishing and maintaining effective, high quality, off-campus graduate programs.

1. The offering of off-campus programs should be consistent with the dynamic nature of the institution. This may include meeting the educational needs of the surrounding community, serving a specific professional population, or furthering advanced teaching and research in the most effective location.

2. Graduate degrees should be offered only in areas where academic strengths already exist on campus and where the institution can provide adequate support in cognate areas.

3. Proposals for new or revised off-campus programs should be approved through the institution's existing curriculum or program review process, which should include a thorough evaluation by the graduate dean. Standards for off-campus programs should be commensurate with those of on-campus offerings, with an equally stringent, regular evaluation process.

4. Before deciding to offer an off-campus graduate program, the institution should conduct a thorough assessment including societal need, relevance to the mission of the institution; academic and administrative impact on the main campus; student demand, fiscal viability, geographical competition; faculty interest and availability, and the availability of adequate facilities and educational resources.

5. Admission criteria should be the same as those used by the institution for its on-campus programs. Degree-seeking students should demonstrate high academic attainment at the undergraduate level, knowledge of subject matter prerequisite to their graduate education, and a potential for the successful pursuit of graduate study.

6. Whenever possible, off-campus programs and courses should be taught by regular full-time faculty, preferably as a part of their assigned teaching load. Adjunct faculty should be used only when regular faculty are not available or when they possess particular knowledge or expertise.

7. While sharing the same academic standards as on-campus programs, off-campus programs should be sensitive to the specific characteristics of the target student population, e.g., the need to schedule classes around work assignments, the usefulness of remote telecommunications, and student interest in specific academic topics or practical applications.

8. Off-campus graduate programs require especially careful academic advisement, delivered at sites and times convenient to students. Academic advisors should be assigned to all students at the time of admission and should meet with students regularly. Students with a particular academic interest should be linked with faculty with similar interests. Advisors should also keep close contact with on-campus offices for any changes or clarifications in policy or degree requirements.

9. Special efforts should be made to insure that library, computer, and other academic resources are adequate and easily accessible. This may involve 1) establishing specialized libraries and computer labs at the off-campus site; 2) making formal agreements with nearby public, private, or university libraries or computer facilities for special use by these students; and 3) providing students with on-line access to bibliographical search services and inter-library loan programs, as well as electronic links to campus computer facilities. In most cases, a combination of these approaches is necessary to provide the intellectual resources needed for graduate study.

Reprinted by permission of the Council of Graduate Schools, One Dupont Circle, N.W., Suite 430, Washington, DC 20036-1173.

APPENDIX C:
GRE AND GMAT
PREPARATION AIDS

SELECTED GRE PREPARATION AIDS

Brownstein, S. C., Weiner, M., & Green, S. W. (1994). *Barron's: How to prepare for the GRE* (11th ed.). Hauppauge, NY: Barron's.

Burgess, P. S., Rozmiarek, E. J., & Weinfeld, M. (1996). *Peterson's GRE success*. Princeton, NJ: Peterson's.

Educational Testing Service. (1996). *GRE: Practicing to take the general test* (9th ed.). Princeton, NJ: Educational Testing Service.

Martinson, T. H. (1995). *Arco: GRE supercourse*. New York: Macmillan.

Robinson, A., & Katzman, J. (1996). *The Princeton review: Cracking the GRE* (1997 ed.). New York: Random House.

Vlk, S. (1996). *The GRE for dummies* (2nd ed.). Foster City, CA: IDG.

ORDERING INFORMATION

For information about the GRE, write to:

Graduate Record Examinations
Educational Testing Service
P.O. Box 6000
Princeton, NJ 08541-6000

Ask for a free copy of the *General Test Descriptive Booklet.*
(This is also usually available through a university's Graduate
School and Office of Career Planning and Placement.)

SELECTED GMAT PREPARATION AIDS

Baron, B., & Downey, E., et al. (1996). *Kaplan: GMAT all-in-one.* New York: Bantam
Doubleday Dell.
Behrens, S. J., Gandhi-Schwatlo, N., & Kirle, B., et al. (1996). *Peterson's: GMAT success.*
Princeton, NJ: Peterson's.
Martz, G., Katzman, J., & Robinson, A. (1996). *The Princeton review: Cracking the GMAT.*
New York: Random House.

For information about the GMAT, write to:

GMAT Test Administration Service
Educational Testing Service, 21V
Princeton, NJ 08541
Fax: 609-520-1092

APPENDIX D:
FINANCIAL AID SOURCES

Cassidy, D. J. (1995). *Dan Cassidy's worldwide graduate scholarship directory* (4th ed.). Franklin Lakes, NJ: Career Press.

Leider, R. (1985). *Lovejoy's guide to financial aid.* New York: Monarch.

McWade, P. (1993). *Financing graduate school: How to get the money you need for your graduate school education.* Princeton, NJ: Peterson's Guides.

Peterson's guide for grants for graduate and postdoctoral study. (1995). Princeton, NJ: Peterson's.

Schlacter, G. A. (1987). *How to find out about financial aid: A guide to over 700 directories listing scholarships, fellowships, loans, grants, awards, internships.* Los Angeles: Reference Service Press.

WORLD WIDE WEB SITES

Mark Kantrowitz's Comprehensive Financial Aid Information Website.

http://www.cs.cmu.edu/afs/cs/user/mkant/Public/FinAid/finaid.html

(also call 1-800-4-fed-aid)

▓ U.S. Government Sites

Marvel.10c.gov/GovernmentInformation/InformationByAgency
ericir/syr.edu/InternetGuides&Directories

INDEX

ABOUT THE AUTHOR

Von Pittman is Director of the Center for Independent Study at the University of Missouri-Columbia, a position he accepted as this book was being published. Previously, he was Associate Dean of Continuing Education at the University of Iowa. He has developed and administered degree programs for working adults and other part-time students, both on and off campus, for nearly two decades, at four major state universities. A member of the graduate faculties in the colleges of education at the Universities of Iowa and Missouri, he regularly teaches courses in the fields of continuing education and distance education. He has published numerous articles and book chapters on the subjects of adult students, teaching at a distance, and the history of continuing education.